Producer of the Living, Eater of the Dead: Revealing Tlaltecuhtli, the Two-Faced Aztec Earth

Lucia Henderson

BAR International Series 1649
2007

Published in 2019 by
BAR Publishing, Oxford

BAR International Series 1649

Producer of the Living, Eater of the Dead: Revealing Tlaltecuhtli, the Two-Faced Aztec Earth

ISBN 9781407300832 paperback
ISBN 9781407331195 e-book

DOI https://doi.org/10.30861/9781407300832

A catalogue record for this book is available from the British Library

This book is available at www.barpublishing.com

BAR Publishing is the trading name of British Archaeological Reports (Oxford) Ltd. British Archaeological Reports was first incorporated in 1974 to publish the BAR Series, International and British. In 1992 Hadrian Books Ltd became part of the BAR group. This volume was originally published by Archaeopress in conjunction with British Archaeological Reports (Oxford) Ltd / Hadrian Books Ltd, the Series principal publisher, in 2007. This present volume is published by BAR Publishing, 2019.

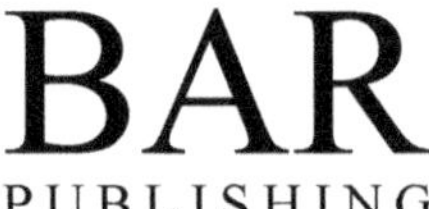

BAR titles are available from:

BAR Publishing
122 Banbury Rd, Oxford, OX2 7BP, UK
EMAIL info@barpublishing.com
PHONE +44 (0)1865 310431
FAX +44 (0)1865 316916
www.barpublishing.com

Dedication

In Memory of Vogtie,
Loving and Wonderful Man,
Whose Flowers, Whose Songs
Will Always Remain an Inspiration.

Will I have to go like the flowers that perish?
Will nothing remain of my name?
Nothing of my fame here on earth?
At least my flowers, at least my songs!
Earth is the region of the fleeting moment.
Is it also thus in the place
Where in some way one lives?
Is there joy there, is there friendship?
Or is it only here on earth
We come to know our faces?

(Matos Moctezuma and Solís 2002:120)

Acknowledgements

This study, which began as an M.A. Thesis for the University of California at San Diego, would not have been possible without the advice, insights, and recommendations of many wonderful people. First, I owe a heartfelt thanks to all of my UCSD mentors and professors – especially Grant Kester, Geoffrey Braswell, Roberto Tejada, and Elizabeth Newsome—and, particularly, to Rhonda Taube, a backbone of support, guidance, and counsel. I was equally fortunate to have the aid and insight of Karl Taube and Eduardo Douglas at the University of California, Riverside, both of whom guided the current study not only in its Master's format, but in developing and transforming it into its current state. I am deeply indebted to them for their time and endless good advice, without which this work would have been difficult indeed. For help in all things Nahuatl, I would also like to thank Jonathan Amith for his patient definitions, clarifications, and explanations. Last but not least, I would like to thank my family and friends for their support, especially my mother, whose constant editorial commentary prevented not only split infinitives, but run-ons and fragments as well.

Most of the drawings presented here are by the author, but I would like to acknowledge all of the people and institutions that have allowed me to reproduce their photographs and illustrations. In a work such as this, the visual element is crucial, so many thanks to all who have made forging that visual connection easier.

Finally, I am deeply grateful to the folks at Archaeopress, whose patience and flexibility have so greatly eased the birth of this work, my very first elephant.

Contents

Part I: Introduction

We live HERE on the earth (stamping the mud floor)
we are all fruits of the earth
the earth sustains us
we grow here, on the earth and lower
and when we die we wither in the earth
we are ALL FRUITS of the earth (stamping the mud floor).

Prayer by the Nahua of San Miguel[1]

Though mentioned in many publications on Aztec art, Tlaltecuhtli,[2] the anthropomorphic version of the Aztec earth, is rarely discussed in depth. Among the numerous Aztec gods, Tlaltecuhtli is particularly difficult to understand, not only because so many variations of the deity are displayed in Aztec iconography, but also because images are most often carved on the undersides of stone objects, out of the sight of both the eyes of viewers and the cameras of catalogers. Despite their relative invisibility to the observer, however, these stone reliefs are "...among the most sophisticated and intricately carved in the whole range of Aztec art" (Nicholson and Quiñones Keber 1983:61). This mastery of form and media is especially remarkable when one recalls the fact that so many of these reliefs, found underneath objects, were never meant to be viewed by anyone or anything other than the earth itself.

These sculpted images of Tlaltecuhtli, in all their many different manifestations, form the basis of the current study. As *teixiptla*, these reliefs were not merely representations of the earth, but embodied the divinity of the earth itself (see Lopéz Austín 1990:138; Houston and Stuart 1996:297). As López Austín states, "There is such a resemblance between image and god that some visible forms charged with sacred power are considered to be gods themselves" (1990:138). Indeed, supernatural forces had a real, physical quality for the Aztecs, "For the Nahuatl man, some of the supernatural beings had a reality as present, as immediate, as daily as he could capture through his senses. The supernatural was judged to be material, potentially visible, tangible, and audible" (López Austín 1988:383). A study of these images, the receptacles the Aztecs created to house the divine substance and power of Tlaltecuhtli, thus reveals the face and the body of the earth itself. Such an analysis also clarifies the manner in which the Aztecs situated themselves *vis à vis* the earth, the physical body of their universe, and the supernatural deity who governed it.

There were several Aztec world models. At times, for instance, the earth was seen as the back of a giant crocodile floating in the midst of the sea. As is recorded in the *Historia de los Mexicanos por sus pinturas*, the gods at the world's beginning created water and within it "...a large fish, like a caiman, that they called Cipactli, and from this fish they made the earth..."[3] (Garibay 1973:25). Another prevalent world model was *cemanahuac*, an island surrounded by water. Finally, there was Tlaltecuhtli, a uniquely anthropomorphic conception of the earth. Unlike other Mexican cultures, whose open-jawed earths can be seen in the Borgia group and Mixtec codices, the Aztecs envisioned their earth with a full human body (see Gutiérrez Solana 1983:20). It is therefore important to study the details of this body as a first step in locating the deity in the Aztec ideological world.

The human body and the body of the earth were often equated in the Nahuatl language. In many incantations, for instance, the human body was called *chicomoztoc*, because the seven wombs of the earth mother were seen as analogous to the seven openings of the human body (López Austín 1988:163). The human body and its soft tissues at times were even called "the earth, the mud" ("*in tlallotl, in zoquiotl*") (Ibid.). As López Austín (1988) argues, the human body was both a world model and vessel of divine energy. It embodied the overarching structure of the universe, the hierarchical distinctions between social classes, and the individual life forces of the soul like the *tonalli* and the *teyolia*. That Tlaltecuhtli was conceived of as an anthropomorphic being, then, links the earth body to all of the frameworks within which the Aztecs sought to organize and understand their society and cosmos.

The physical, anchored reality of *terra firma* is often overlooked in studies about Aztec worldview and cosmology. As a result, the earth as a corporeal being has, in many ways, been glossed over as a key factor in the way in which the Aztecs understood their world. Because

[1] Recorded by Tim Knab (quoted in Broda 1987:107).

[2] Though authors often disagree on whether the proper spelling is "teuctli" or "tecuhtli," the latter is used here. Since the "uc" and "cu" historically stand for a labialized "k" value (what would be spelled "kw" in modern transcriptions), the spellings are technically equivalent (Jonathan Amith, pers. comm. 2006). "Tlaltecuhtli" is used here because it is not only the most commonly used variant of the deity's name, but also most closely approximates the phonetic value of the Nahuatl word "tekwtli."

[3] All translations from Spanish sources are by the author.

Tlaltecuhtli is so rarely discussed in depth, references to the deity are often contradictory or inconsistent. Tlaltecuhtli, for instance, is regarded equally as male, female, or ambiguously gendered, while arguments about the number of iconographic variants of the deity range from two to four. This study attempts to resolve these contradictions by laying down a strong, detailed, and heavily supported iconographic framework. In this way, I hope to illuminate the significance behind images of Tlaltecuhtli, to clarify the role this "Earth Lord" or "earth monster" played in the Aztec world, and thereby help future researchers face questions about the earth in a more confident manner.

To What End? Outline of Purpose and Arguments

The purpose of this volume is multi-fold. First and foremost, I aim to demonstrate not only that there were two main Tlaltecuhtli variants (here referred to as "Tlaltecuhtli 1" (Figures 1-5) and "Tlaltecuhtli 2" (Figures 6-7)), but that the first of these was female and the second male. Second, the current work enumerates and discusses the various iconographic elements borne by each of these variants in an effort to elucidate their meanings and symbolism. Finally, this article aims to compile not only the arguments and sources relevant to studies of Tlaltecuhtli, but also, for the first time, all known published images of the deity.

In this study I focus specifically on representations of Tlaltecuhtli rather than broader imagery of the earth or of earth goddesses in general. Tlaltecuhtli, the anthropomorphic version of the Aztec earth, was, for the most part, rendered in stone reliefs found in and around the Aztec capital of Tenochtitlan. According to Nicholson (1954:166), Seler was probably the first to recognize these images of squatting creatures beneath stone boxes and *cuauhxicalli* as "Tlaltecuhtli in the guise of a great monster-toad." A number of efforts to describe and classify Tlaltecuhtli imagery have followed, including works by Gutiérrez Solana (1983), Baquedano (1988), Baquedano and Orton (1990), and, most notably, those of Nicholson (1954, 1967,1972) and Matos Moctezuma (1997). The method and conclusions of the present study are most closely tied to these final two authors. Two main points, however, differentiate the current work from its predecessors. First, unlike Nicholson (1954, 1967, 1972), who argues for three Tlaltecuhtli variants, and Matos Moctezuma (1997), who argues for four, I conclude that there are only two main Tlaltecuhtli variants.[4] The new classification combines into one category (Tlaltecuhtli 1) the "anthropomorphic female" and "zoomorphic female" groups of Matos Moctezuma, also known as female head and jaw variants in Nicholson's work. Secondly, though the current classification, like that of Matos Moctezuma, does draw a distinction between male figures without goggles (Tlaltecuhtli 2) and with goggles. I consider the latter category, which is seen in only two relief images (Figures 25a-b), to be more closely allied with other images of deities combined with Tlaltecuhtli (like Tlalchitonatiuh (Fig.8), Quetzalcoatl-Tlaltecuhtli (Fig.30), and Itzpapalotl-Tlaltecuhtli (Fig.12a)). Therefore, such figures are classified as "deity variants," related to, though located outside the boundaries of, the two main Tlaltecuhtli categories.

Because this two-part classification of Tlaltecuhtli imagery relies so heavily on gender identifications (Tlaltecuhtli 1 as female and Tlaltecuhtli 2 as male), the current study also makes an effort to clarify and dispel the contradictory arguments about Tlaltecuhtli's gender that abound in the literature. Though often referred to as an ambiguously gendered or a combined gender figure, Tlaltecuhtli was, in reality, a deity with two distinct manifestations. The first of these, Tlaltecuhtli 1, was female and represented the face of the Mexica earth. The second, Tlaltecuhtli 2, was a male version of the earth who referenced the deities of the predecessors of the Aztec Empire, especially Teotihuacan and the Gulf Coast. As will be discussed, I believe this doubling of the earth represents an effort on the part of the Aztecs to reconcile the new gods of their Chichimec identity with the old gods of their Toltec predecessors. In other words, these images of Tlaltecuhtli are a physical manifestation of the Aztec struggle to forge a new personal identity from a multiple ethnic history.

Another crucial aspect of the current study is an analysis of the significance of the details within Tlaltecuhtli imagery. Baquedano and Orton (1990) pave the way for this kind of a study by identifying 145 different iconographic elements present in Tlaltecuhtli iconography. Their study, however, does not discuss the significance of these elements or what their presence or absence from Tlaltecuhtli images means. Klein (1976:57 f.n.1) argues against the relevance of such details in discussions of Tlaltecuhtli imagery: "There is, however, no observable pattern in the distribution of these various attributes which were more or less interchangable [sic]. It is evident, therefore, that there was little formal distinction made between the various aspects of the female earth monster…" A close analysis of the details of Tlaltecuhtli forms, however, indicates that a distinct pattern exists that determines which items are associated with which Tlaltecuhtli variants. Articles like coyote tails,

[4] Nicholson's (1954, 1967,1972) three-part Tlaltecuhtli classification is comprised of the following categories: an open maw filled with teeth (Figures 1-3), an upside-down human face (Figures 4-5), and a "Tlalocoid" face (Figures 6-7, 25a-b). Matos Moctezuma (1997), on the other hand, argues for four categories of images: zoomorphic females (Figures 1-3), anthropomorphic females (Figures 4-5), anthropomorphic males (Figures 6-7), and Tlalocoid figures (Figure 25a-b). The main difference between the work of Nicholson and Matos Moctezuma is that the latter separates "anthropomorphic males" from "Tlalocoid" figures, categories combined under Nicholson's "Tlalocoid" classification. Matos Moctezuma's anthropomorphic males wear the Teotihuacan Storm God headdress and mouth mask but lack goggles. "Tlalocoid" figures, on the other hand, are seen as more directly allied with Tlaloc imagery, wearing the headdress, mouthpiece, and goggles of this Aztec rain god.

spotted paper banners, and skulls lashed onto elbows and knees are not equally distributed among Tlaltecuhtli categories or subcategories, and their specific allocation indicates that each is meaningful in its own right.

The final purpose of the current study is to act as a potential database for future scholars. First, because statements and arguments about Tlaltecuhtli, especially the deity's gender, are so often made without supporting evidence, I have been as thorough as possible with bibliographic references. Second, and perhaps more importantly, I have compiled, for the first time, all known published images of Tlaltecuhtli.[5] By doing so, I hope to make this study a starting point, an initial step towards a better understanding of the Aztec earth. By gathering in one place all known images of Tlaltecuhtli as well as offering a thorough analysis of the details by which this deity was described and expressed in Aztec iconography, the current work aims to act as an armature for future studies and scholars.

In sum, though the primary argument of the current study is that the Aztec earth had two distinct faces (one male and one female), an equally important objective is that it will serve as a resource for future research. That the Aztecs divided their earth into two distinct entities, one male and one female, one ancient and one new, has serious implications in terms of the way in which this culture viewed its position on the earth, in the cosmos, and in history. Perhaps more importantly, however, such conclusions indicate that Aztec conceptions of the earth not only were shaped by, but may also have actively shaped Aztec notions of individual and group identity. It follows that further study of Aztec earth imagery can bring us closer to understanding not only the overall Aztec worldview, but also the more personal struggles through which this worldview was formed.

A Summary of Tlaltecuhtli Imagery:

Representations of Tlaltecuhtli often appear so various as to defy attempts at categorization. This frequently fosters a feeling that the iconography of the earth must be approached in an almost instinctual way—that intuition is the only means of determining which images do, in fact, represent the earth. What is needed is an establishment of parameters that designate both the boundary around Tlaltecuhtli imagery in general, and also those boundaries that differentiate Tlaltecuhtli variants from one another. In other words, there must be a two-tiered means of categorization. First, the question of what characteristics are shared by all representations of Tlaltecuhtli creates a broad category of earth imagery, setting the rules by which a corpus of comparative images can be formed. Second, a more detailed definition of each Tlaltecuhtli group, 1 and 2 (see Appendix 1), allows for a more specific division among Tlaltecuhtli types. When addressed with such an analytical scheme, Tlaltecuhtli imagery easily separates into individual forms. The component parts of these forms becomes clear, and what once appeared chaotic begins to take shape as a formally structured iconographic system.

In this study, in order to be considered a depiction of Tlaltecuhtli, an image must be two-dimensional, depicted in a straight-on view, and show the deity in the splayed body position known as the "hocker" position. The first of these, two-dimensionality, may also be seen as determined by media, for full-bodied representations of Tlaltecuhtli are only found in the Aztec codices, in stone reliefs, and on one inscribed femur from Colhuacan (Figure 1d) (see Graulich 1988:398; Von Winning 1968:f.396/397). In the Aztec codices, one only finds images of Tlaltecuhtli 1a, at times comprising part of Tlalchitonatiuh (Figure 8). Due to the lack of variety in codex depictions of Tlaltecuhtli, however, as well as the fact that no inarguably pre-Conquest Aztec codices are currently known, the current study considers such imagery secondary to stone relief depictions of the deity. Like codex images, Tlaltecuhtli representations in stone are always two-dimensional and, generally speaking, are carved on the undersides of stone boxes, beneath *cuauhxicalli*, or as panel faces.

It is true that the preceding outline of general Tlaltecuhtli imagery may be deemed too vague to be practically useful. One must therefore emphasize that, in addition to the three characteristics described above (two dimensionality, a straight-on view, and the hocker position), Tlaltecuhtli imagery must exhibit the more specific features of either Tlaltecuhtli 1 or Tlaltecuhtli 2. These features are so systematic in their arrangement that one can easily differentiate between the two. A summary of these features follows, while a complete list is also shown in table form as Appendix 1.

All images of the female earth (Figures 1-5), Tlaltecuhtli 1, display toothy, masked elbows and knees, a skull and crossbones skirt, *malinalli* hair, clawed hands and feet, and striated bracelets and anklets. This category can be further subdivided into Tlaltecuhtli 1a and 1b head variants, the former marked by a gaping mouth, and the latter marked by an upside-down female head. Tlaltecuhtli 1a, the toothy mouth variant, is seen in both frontal and dorsal poses, the first distinguishable by a skull back ornament and apron (Figure 1) and the second marked by a central *chalchihuitl* or *ollin* sign (Figure 2). The Tlaltecuhtli 1a category also includes the "1a knife variant," a formulaic rendition of the deity found on the undersides of *cuauhxicalli* sacrificial vessels (Figure 3). Tlaltecuhtli 1b (Figures 4-5), which exhibits an upside-down female head, is only shown in the dorsal pose and

[5] In order to clarify the iconography of these images, most have been drawn by the author. It is important to note, however, that these drawings were made from photographs, many of which, unfortunately, were of poor quality. As a result, though they do offer readers the clearest images of the monuments that are currently available, they should not be considered definitive.

displays spotted paper banners and coyote tails attached to her wrists and legs. Certain Tlaltecuhtli 1 variants display war or sacrificial banners (spotted and plain) as well as coyote tails tied to the wrists. Some also clasp skulls in their hands and feet or wear skulls tied on to their limbs.

In general, Tlaltecuhtli 1 imagery appears to focus on Mexica themes, situating the earth as a female, violated and dismembered for the greater good of humankind. Her iconography emphasizes, above all, warfare, sacrifice, and consumption. Creation, production, and fertility, however, are also referenced, demonstrating the overall Aztec tendency towards oppositional arrangements and the balance of dual forces.

Tlaltecuhtli 2 (Figures 6-7), the male version of the earth, is easily differentiated from Tlaltecuhtli 1 forms. With an upright head wearing a Teotihuacan-style Storm God headdress and mouthpiece, Tlaltecuhtli 2 displays features that are, for the most part, distinct from those of Tlaltecuhtli 1. He wears a large circular shield marked by a quincunx, boots with upturned toes, and a loincloth. His arms are outlined with double scrollwork and his thumbs are shown with claws, though the rest of his fingers are shown in a naturalistic manner. He also carries skulls in his hands and wears skulls tied onto his arms and legs, features shared with some Tlaltecuhtli 1 forms.

Unlike Tlaltecuhtli 1, Tlaltecuhtli 2 references the ancestral earth. His features are drawn from non-Aztec sources, including Teotihuacan and the Gulf Coast, and appear to reference these ancient civilizations as a means of legitimizing Aztec rule. Overall, though war and sacrifice symbolism are present, his imagery is more peaceful than that of Tlaltecuhtli 1, appearing to emphasize the verdant green of the Gulf Coast as well as the fertilizing, watery nature of both the Teotihuacan Storm God as well as the Aztec Tlaloc.

Resolving the Gender Question:

When examining the way in which the Aztecs viewed their earth, one of the main issues that needs resolution is the deity's gender. Discussed, referenced, mentioned, but rarely argued in depth, Tlaltecuhtli's gender remains a contested and contradictory subject in contemporary literature. While some authors describe Tlaltecuhtli as an ambiguously gendered or combined-gender being, others state that the deity is entirely female or male. As gender is so often stated rather than argued, however, it is often difficult for scholars to approach the topic in a confident way. A close analysis of Tlaltecuhtli imagery, however, makes it clear that this deity was in no way ambiguously gendered, but instead was expressed in two forms. The Aztecs had two earths, one male and one female, in which gender markings and distinctions were never combined.

While some authors explicitly reference the ambiguous gender of Tlaltecuhtli (see, for instance, Pasztory 1983; Klein 1980; Gutiérrez Solana 1983; Miller and Taube 1993; Carrera 1979:178; Baquedano 1989:195; etc.), others alternately refer to her as male or female without specifically addressing gender identity (see Arnold 1999). In their editorial comments on the work of Ruiz de Alarcón, for instance, Andrews and Hassig (Ruiz de Alarcón 1984:238) define "Tlalteuctli" as "Lord-of-the-Land," and state, "In classical times, *Tlalteuctli* was an earth god." Though they describe Tlaltecuhtli as male, they acknowledge the contradiction between this identification and that of Ruiz de Alarcón himself, who consistently "…treats *Tlalteuctli* as a feminine entity, addressing her as *nonan* ("my mother," i.e., "my lady")" (Ibid.). Heyden (1971:160), for her part, explains combined genders as a feature of most creator deities, while González Torres uses the term "androgynous" (1985:138) to describe Tlaltecuhtli. A number of authors also use the word "bisexual" to describe Tlaltecuhtli (see, for instance, Fox 1993; Nicholson 1971, 1993; Klein 1980:162; Nicholson and Quiñones Keber 1983:61; Heyden 1971:168), but because this term is so commonly and frequently used to designate sexual preference rather than gender identity, its use is avoided here.

Some authors argue for a fully female identification of Tlaltecuhtli. "As the archetype of fertility, birth, and nurture, she was logically conceived of as a female and a mother" (Klein 1973:71). Throughout Mesoamerica, ethnographic sources demonstrate that the earth and earth deities are generally conceptualized as female. Both contemporary Huichol (see Zingg 1977) and Nahua (see Sandstrom 1991) groups, for instance, discuss the earth and earth deities as, for the most part, female. The Tzotzil are no different: "The Earth is the mother of universal life. She is the most compelling power in the universe. She is the supreme power. All others seem to form part of her or to have proceeded from her depths" (Guiteras-Holmes 1961:189). Worldwide, the earth is often assumed to have a female identity, despite the fact that several notable civilizations, including the Egyptians, believed in a male earth.

A female identity for Tlaltecuhtli is often argued in opposition to the male earth, the crocodilian *cipactli*, from whose primordial form Tlaltecuhtli was conceived. As Brundage argues, "When formed into a primitive version of the earth, this dragon [Cipactli] was generally conceived as female and was known as Tlaltecuhtli, Earth Lady" (1976:31). Klein goes into more detail about the iconographic differences between the two forms. "Both her invariable frontal form and strictly feminine pose thus distinguish [Tlaltecuhtli] clearly from the earth crocodile deity Cipactli, who was regarded as male and who always appears in profile form in two-dimensional Post-Classic images" (1973:70).

When authors argue for the ambiguous gender of Tlaltecuhtli, it is generally on the basis of one of four pieces of evidence that seem to indicate that the deity was, at least partially, conceived of as male. The first is the use of the phrase "father, mother" when addressing Tlaltecuhtli. That such a statement refers to gender ambiguity, however, is refuted by Heyden, who discusses this word pairing as a means of formal address, an honorific rather than an indication of an indistinct gender identity (Durán 1994:59 f.n.2). The second is the description found in the *Histoire du Mechique* which states, "There was a goddess called Tlalteutl, the earth itself, who, according to some, had the figure of a man, while others say that she was a woman" (Garibay 1973:105). It is true that this quote seems to indicate disagreement over whether Tlaltecuhtli was male or female, but there is no indication that the deity was considered a combination or indeterminate blending of the two. Rather than arguing that the deity was ambiguously gendered, this description instead hints at either a separation between those who believed in a male earth and those who believed in a female earth or that there were two earths, one male and one female.

The third argument used by authors to support ambiguous gender is iconographic—the wearing of the male *maxtlatl* loincloth by otherwise female Tlaltecuhtli figures. Images found in the Codex Borbonicus, for instance, appear to show female Tlaltecuhtli figures wearing *maxtlatl* loincloths. As Nicholson (1967) and Klein (1976:55-56 f.n.1) point out, however, these garments are more likely instead the back aprons so often worn by earth goddesses. Dressed in a simplified version of the back apron and skull ornament so frequently used in Aztec art to indicate a female identity, these figures are therefore identifiable as fully female rather than combined- or bi-gendered.

The fourth argument used to support gender ambiguity is generally implicit, often underlying statements rather than explicitly stated as evidence: the translation of "Tlaltecuhtli" as "earth lord" (see Matos Moctezuma 1997). This translation is taken from such Spanish-Nahuatl dictionaries as that of Simeon, who translates "Tlaltecutli" as "Señor de la tierra" (1977:605). Though the gender of Tlaltecuhtli indicated by Simeon is clearly male, it should be understood as a result of the gendering of the Spanish language (in which nouns are always sexed) rather than an innate Nahuatl linguistic marker. Nahuatl is an ungendered language, and though "tecuhtli" is often attached to the names of male deities, it is used for goddesses, like Ilamatecuhtli, as well. As Jonathan Amith notes (pers. comm. 2004), "tecuhtli" might be better understood as a status marker rather than one of gender, referring "...to persons, entities, places, etc. that were in a higher, lordly position over another of the same." Tlaltecuhtli would thus be understood as the highest status of the earth deities. It should also be noted that, for the Spanish, the earth was "la tierra," a feminine entity, and therefore sixteenth-century Spanish accounts that include descriptions of the earth combine masculine translations of "tecuhtli" with a feminine linguistic bias towards the earth, unconsciously designating Tlaltecuhtli as ambiguously gendered.

In iconography, Tlaltecuhtli's gender is very clearly marked. Rather than a figure that combined male and female features, Tlaltecuhtli was an earth conceived of in two ways: one female and one male. When Tlaltecuhtli 1 is shown, the figure is clearly marked as female, generally with a skull back rack or a skull and crossbones skirt. The back ornament in particular is used as an element of female costuming in Aztec art. For example, on the stones of Moctezuma I and Tizoc two female captives wear back skull ornaments with aprons (Figure 10e), while the other male captives on the stone lack these elements. Similarly, on the Fonds Mexicain page 20 the accoutrement of the female *cihuateteo* is distinguished from that of their male *ahuiateteo* counterparts by the skull back ornament and apron (Lehman 1966). Therefore, such skulls and aprons served in Aztec art as a means of differentiating female from male figures. The skull and crossbones skirt is also widely understood to be a female garment, worn by goddesses associated with the earth as well as by the *cihuateteo* and *tzitzimime* (Klein 2000). Statements like "*in tonan, in tota, in tonatiuh in tlaltecutli,*" which translate as "our mother, our father, the sun, the lord of the earth" (Sahagún 1950-82[VI]:12), also support a female identity. Since the sun is an unequivocally male figure, he must represent the "*tota*" part of this invocation, leaving "*tonan*" ("our mother") to Tlaltecuhtli.

While Tlaltecuhtli 1 is clearly marked as female, Tlaltecuhtli 2 (Figures 6-7) is just as clearly male. He wears a male *maxtlatl* and bears no female symbols. His facemask is never seen worn by female deities and neither are his headdress or pointed boots. It is true that, in sixteenth-century literature and myth the Aztec earth that one predominantly encounters is the female earth (see, Ruiz de Alarcón 1984), though this may at times result from the Spanish language gendering process. Nicholson describes this predominance of the female earth as an indication of her greater importance in Aztec worldview:

> ...most of the available evidence suggests that in late pre-Hispanic Central Mexico the earth in general and the earth monster in the *mamazouhticac* position in particular was usually conceived to be female and depicted wearing the costume proper to that sex. A male aspect of this element was also recognized... and occasionally represented in appropriate garb—but was apparently quite subordinate to the more fundamental and pervasive female conception. (Nicholson 1967:87)

The numerous examples of Tlaltecuhtli 2 imagery and the interchangeability between Tlaltecuhtli 1 and 2 forms, however, each of which is shown with equal regularity beneath objects like feathered serpents and monumental figures, indicate that the male earth was just as important as the female earth. More likely than indicating a hierarchical difference between the two forms, the seeming predominance of the female earth in literature and myth may instead be due to the fact that Tlaltecuhtli 2 was a composite of iconography from ancestral cultures. It is therefore possible that the Aztecs did not link it as closely to their origin myths as their more typically Mexica female earth and therefore mentioned it far less often, despite its frequent depiction in sculptured form.

Features Shown by Tlaltecuhtli Variants

	Head			Clawed hands/ feet	Skulls in feet/ hands	Skull back apron	*Chalchihuitl/ ollin* sign on abdomen	Coyote tails on wrists	Banners on legs		Central *kan* shield	Skulls tied on knees/ elbows	Masks on joints	Loin-cloth	Insects in hair
	Jaw	Upside-down	Upright						Plain	With spots					
1a frontal	X	O	O	X	O	O	X	O	O	O	O	O	X	O	O
1a dorsal	X	O	O	X	O	X	O	X	X	O	O	O	X	O	S
1a flint	X	O	O	X	O	X	O	O	O	O	O	X	S	O	O
1b	O	X	O	X	X	X	O	X	O	X	O	S	X	O	S
2	O	O	X	O *	X	O	O	O	O	O	X	X	O	X	O

X= Always
S= Sometimes
O= Never

* Tlaltecuhtli 2 is shown with taloned thumbs only.

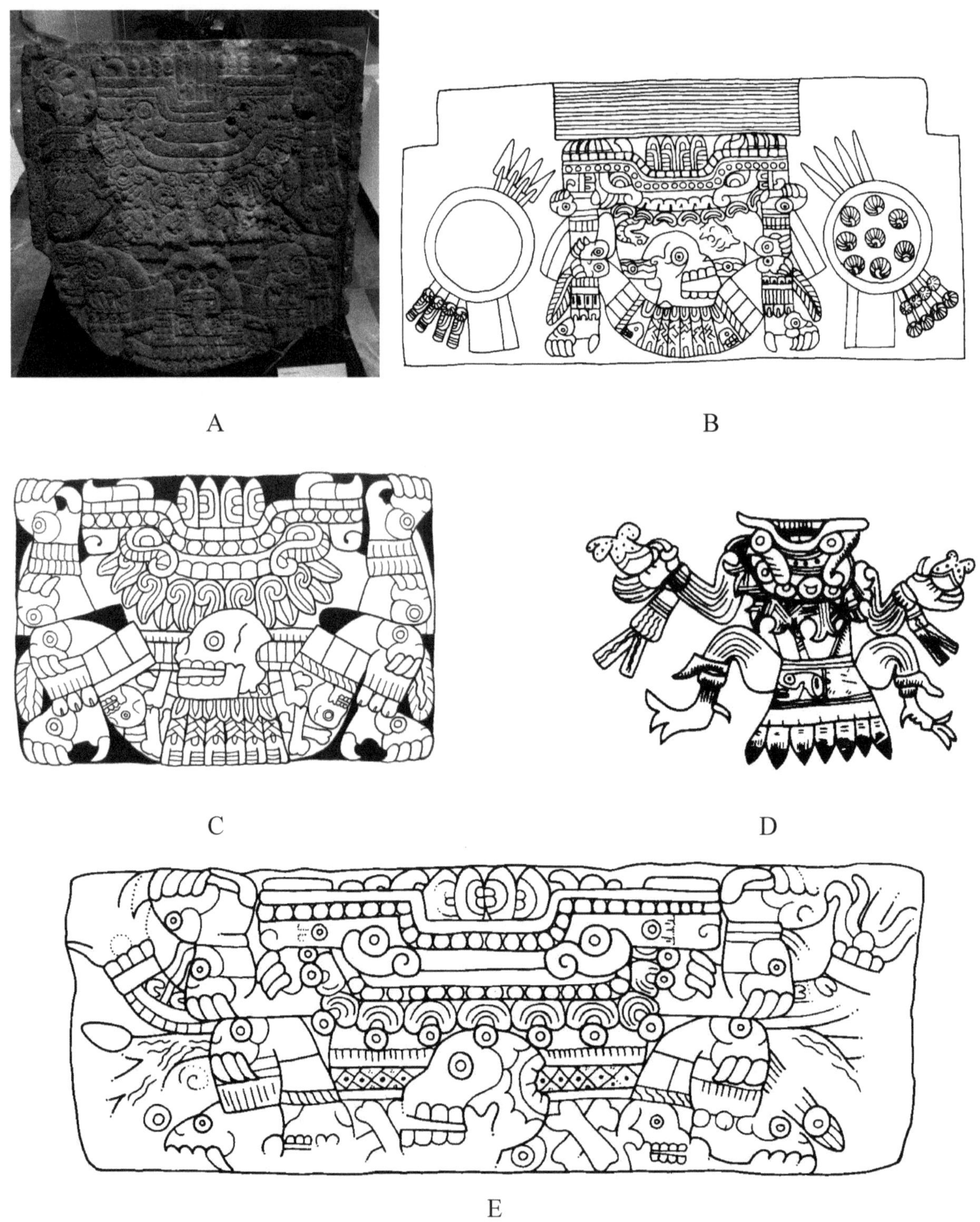

Figure 1: Tlaltecuhtli 1a (dorsal views): a) Base of broken "goddess" (photo by author); b) Seat of Teocalli of Moctezuma (drawing by author after Townsend 1979:f.22a); c) Offering box marked with One Cipactli on the interior (Taube 1993:36); d) Inscription from a human femur from Culhuacan (drawing by author after Von Winning 1968:f.396/397); e) Side of Stone of Four Creations (drawing by author after Nicholson and Quiñones Keber 1983:42).

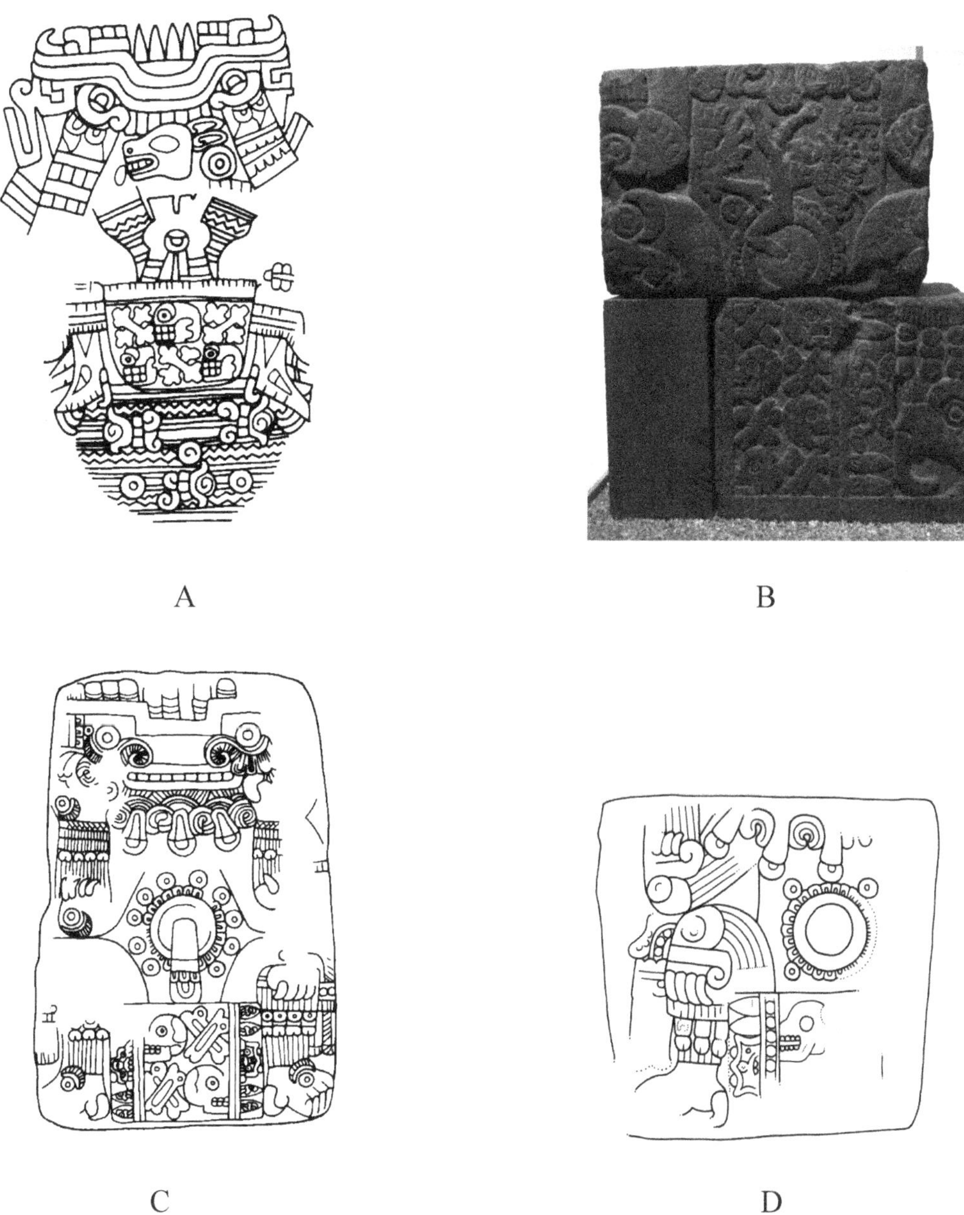

Figure 2: Tlaltecuhtli 1a (frontal views): a) Base of the Bilimek pulque vessel (drawing by author after Pasztory 1983:pl.282); b) Relief showing birth of Tezcatlipoca (photo by author. See Covarrubias 1957:f.140 for reconstruction drawing); c) Relief panel (drawing by author after Pasztory 1983:pl.98); d) Relief panel fragment (drawing by author after Nicholson 1967:f.5).

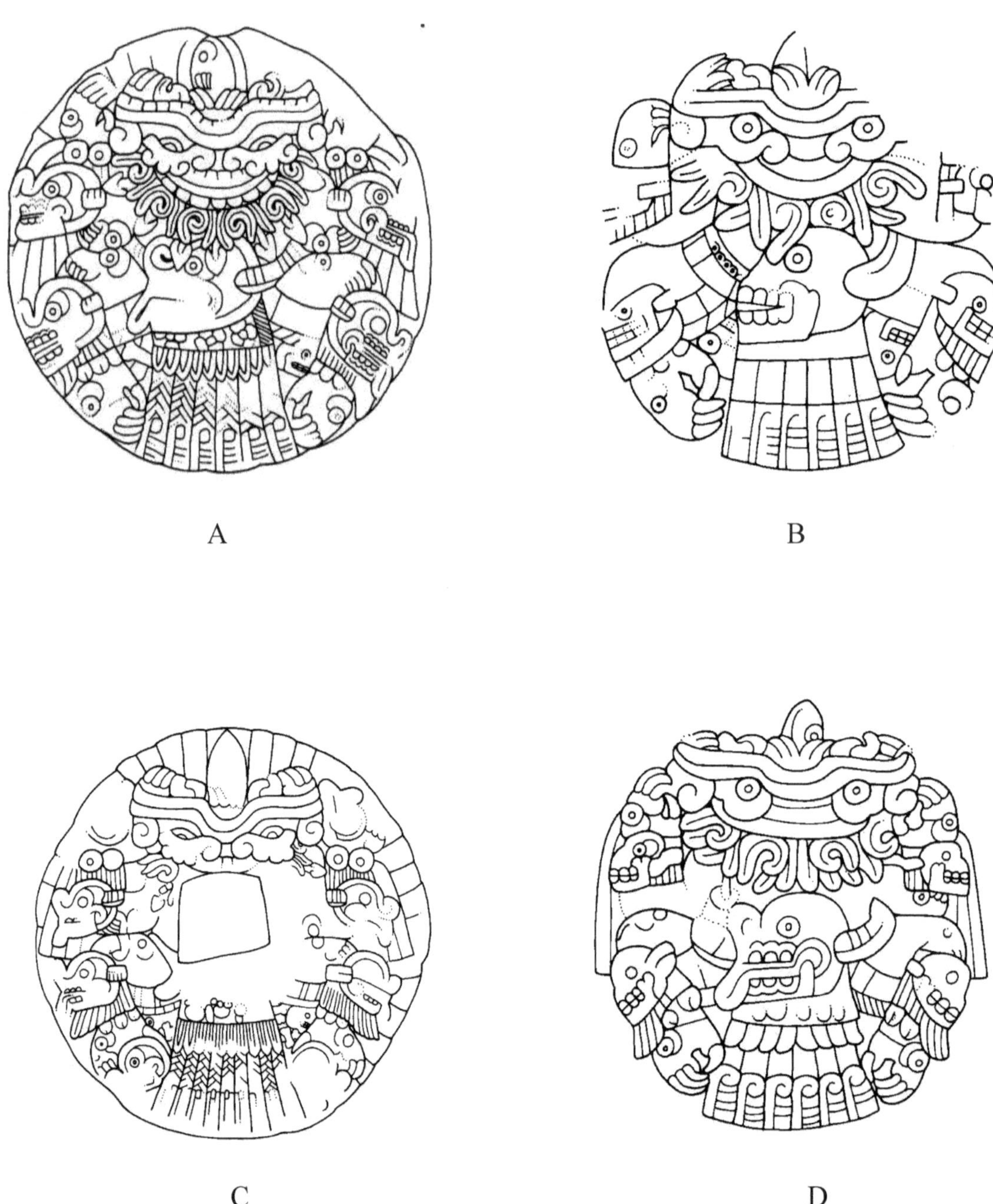

Figure 3: Tlaltecuhtli 1a "Knife Variant": a) Base of feathered serpent (drawing by author after Pasztory 1983:pl.216); b) *Cuauhxicalli* (drawing by author after Alcina Franch, et al. 1992:307); c) Possible base of feathered serpent (drawing by author after Ibid.:f.171); d) *Cuauhxicalli* (drawing by author after Ibid.:f.53).

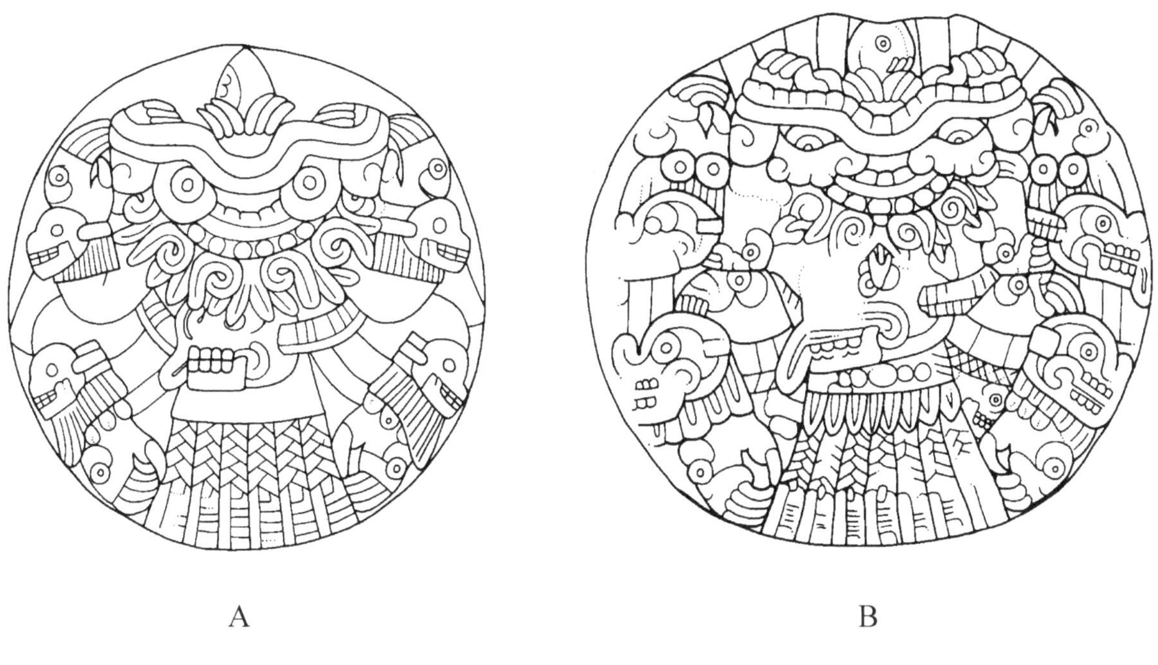

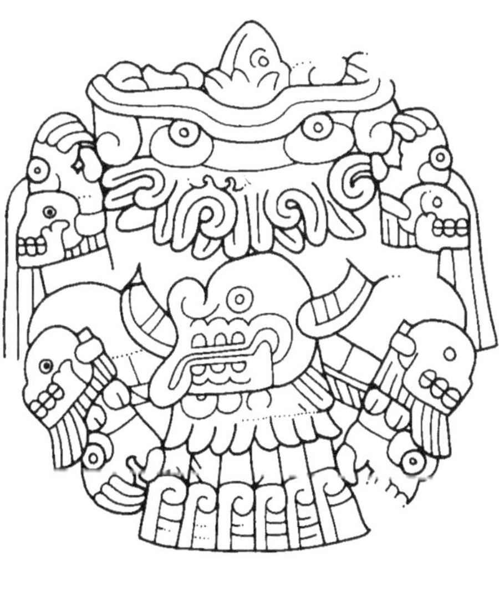

Figure 3 (cont'd): e) *Cuauhxicalli* (drawing by author after Pasztory 1983:Colorplate 48); f) Object unknown (drawing by author after Gutiérrez Solana 1983:f.205); g) *Cuauhxicalli* (drawing by author after Alcina Franch, et al. 1992:306).

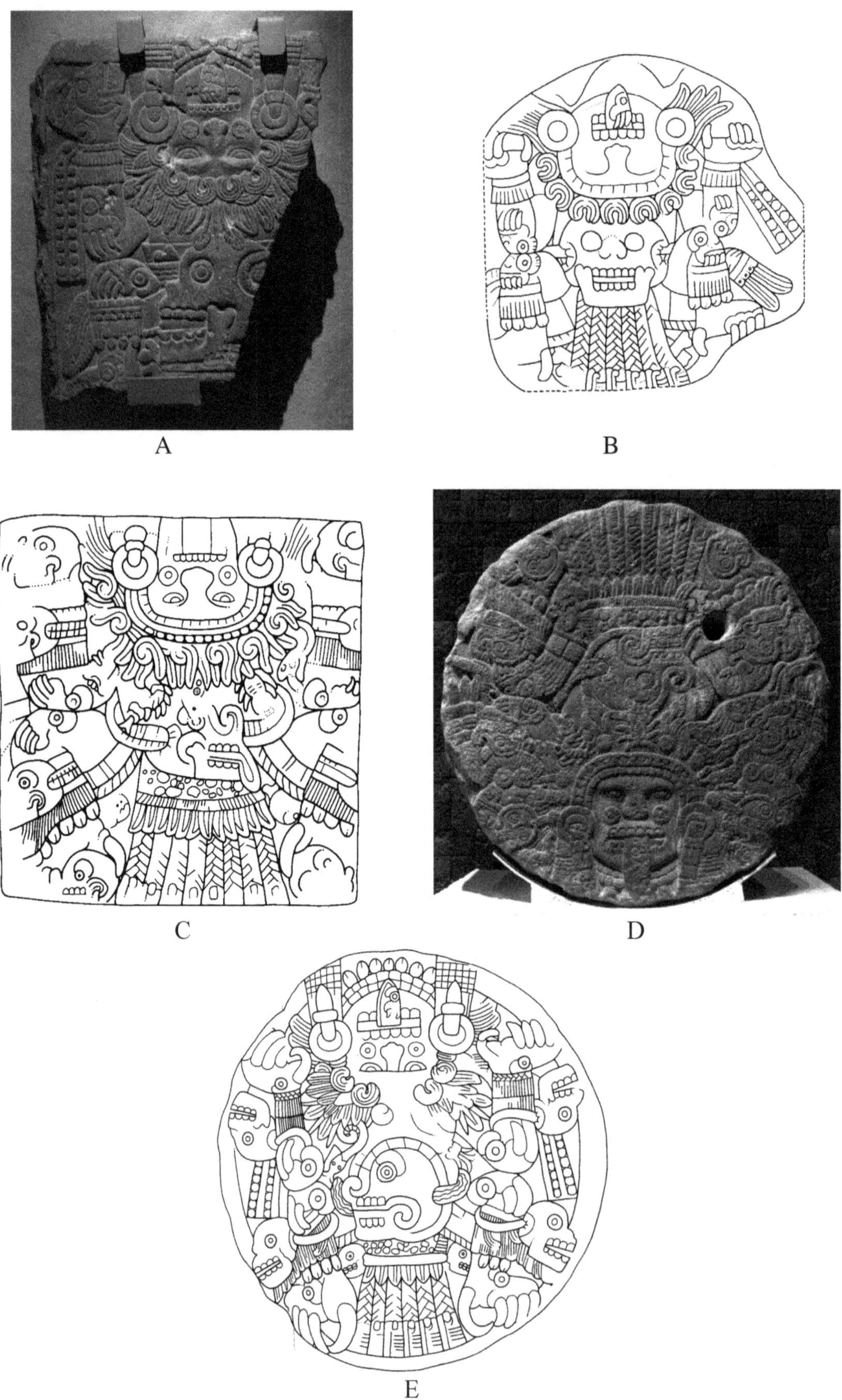

Figure 4: Tlaltecuhtli 1b: a) Relief panel (photo by author); b) Underside of unknown object (drawing by author after Gutiérrez Solana 1983:f.174); c) Underside of Spanish column base (drawing by author after Ibid.:f.175); d) Base of offertory vessel (drawing by author after Pasztory 1983:pl.37); e) Object unknown (drawing by author after Von Winning 1968:f.389).

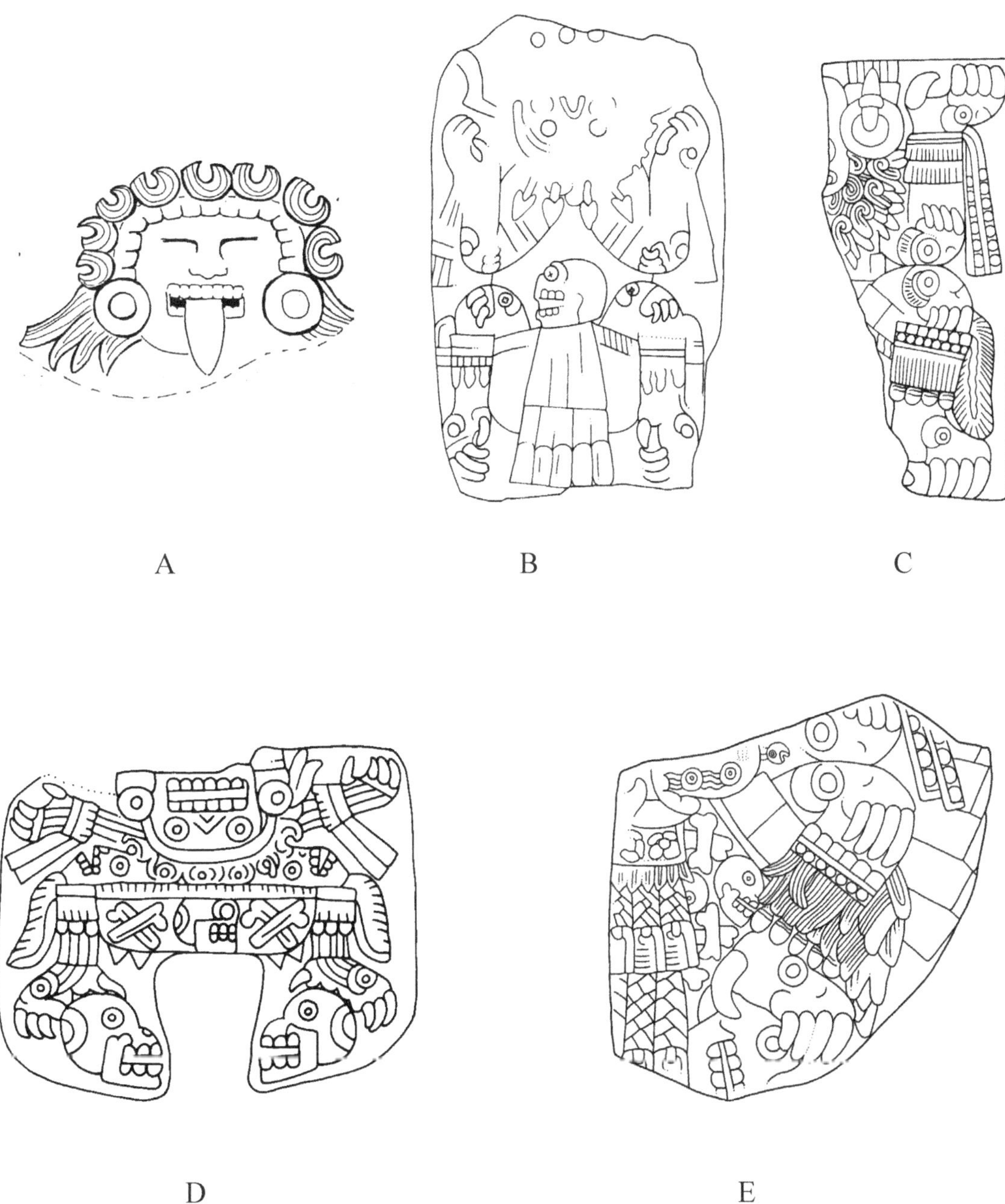

Figure 5: Tlaltecuhtli 1b (continued): a) Box fragment (Peterson 1983:f.13); b) Alabaster relief panel (drawing by author after Matos Moctezuma 1997:f.21); c) Bottom of box (drawing by author after Baquedano 1984:f.59); d) Base of Stuttgart statuette (drawing by author after Klein 1976:f.7); e) Fragment from base of feathered serpent (drawing by author after Townsend 1979:29).

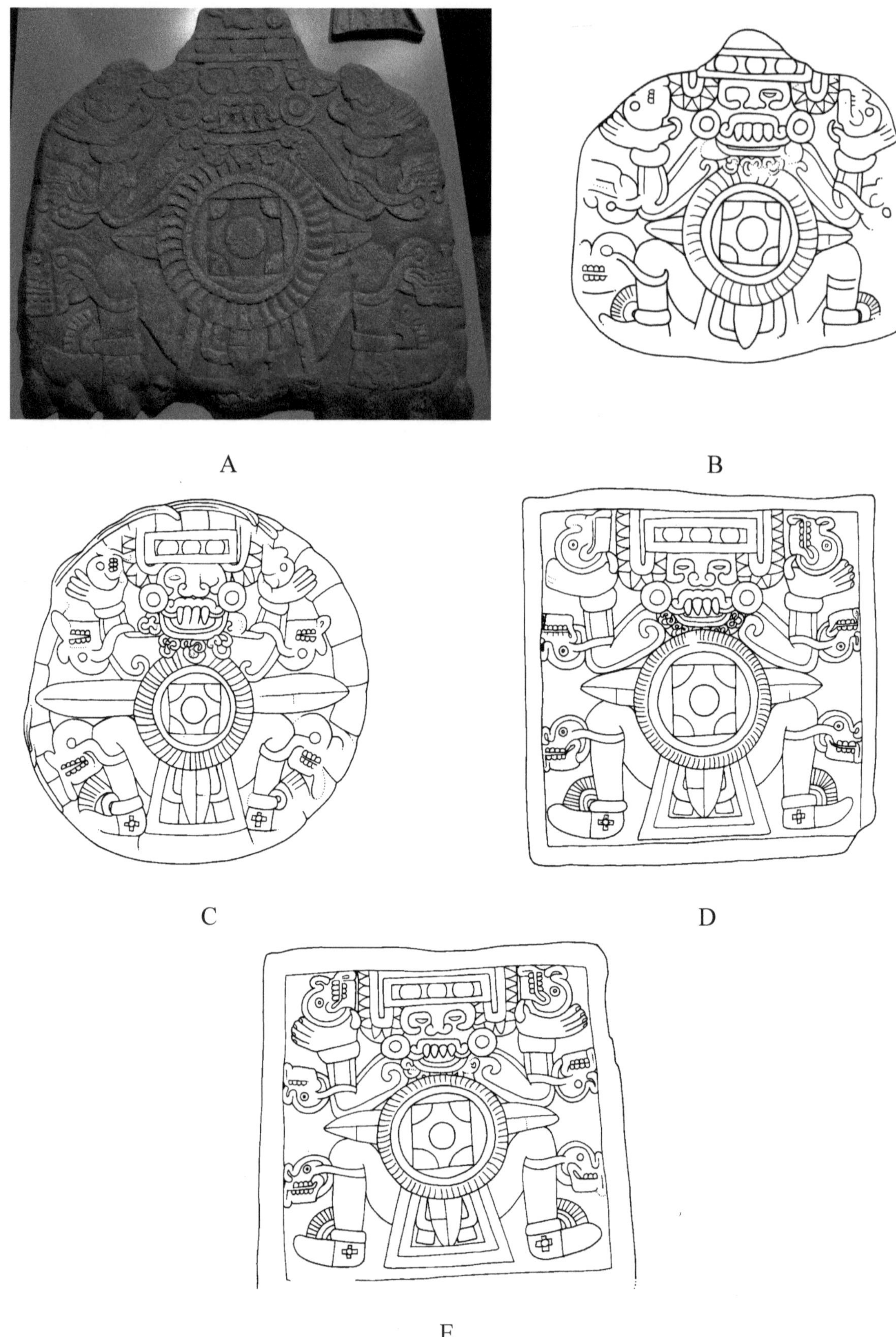

Figure 6: Tlaltecuhtli 2: a) Base of Coatlique (photo by author); b) Base of Yollotlicue (drawing by author after Nicholson 1967:f.8); c) Base of plumed serpent (drawing by author after Pasztory 1983:pl.117); d) Cube base (drawing by author after Solís 2004:f.87); e) Possible cube base (drawing by author after Alcina Franch, et al. 1992:f.95).

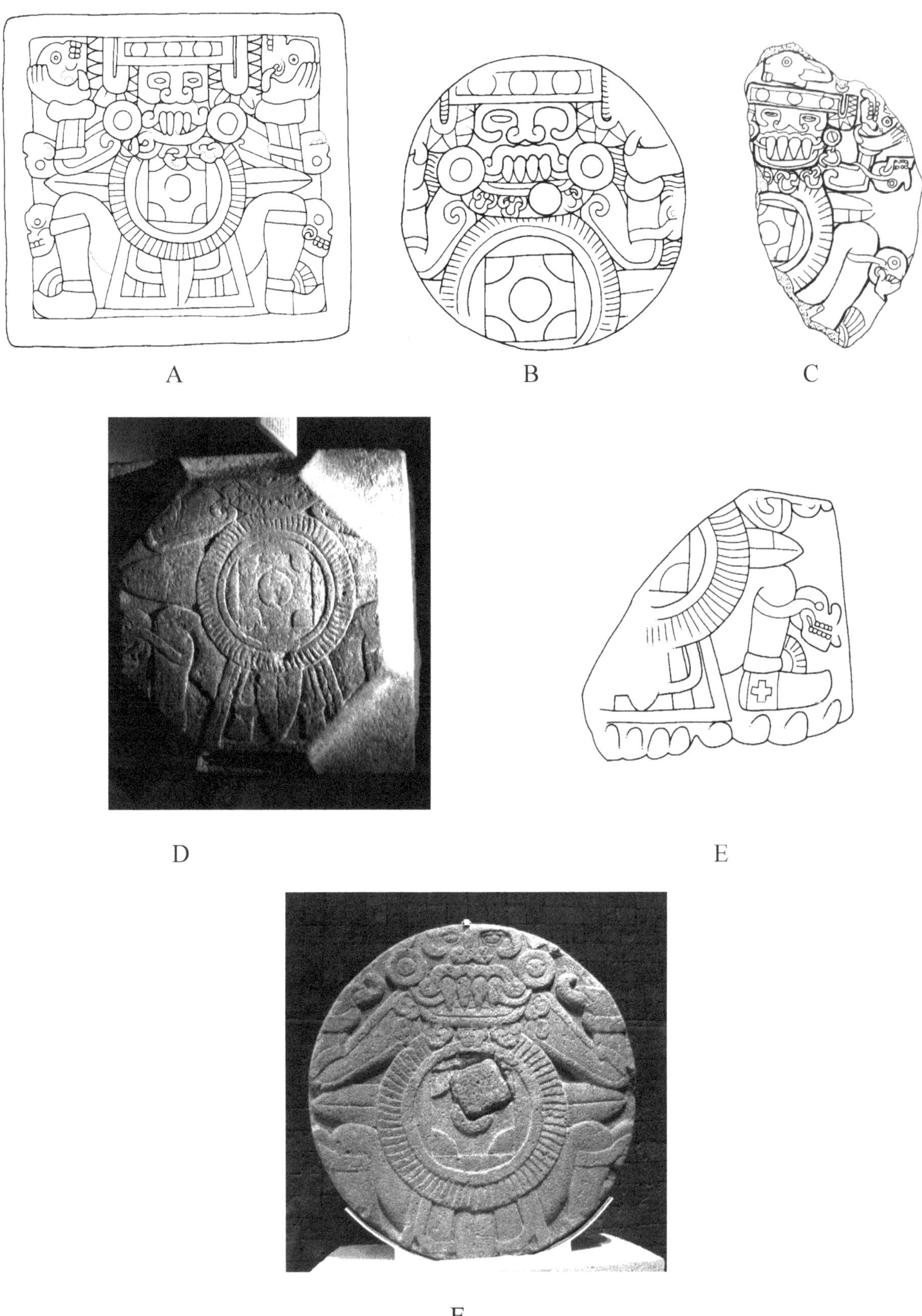

Figure 7: Tlaltecuhtli 2 (continued): a) Possible cube base (drawing by author after Nicholson and Quiñones Keber 1983:12); b) Recarved millstone (drawing by author after Museo Nacional de Antropología, Mexico City 11-5354); c) Fragment from base of *cihuateotl* (Batres 1900:f.6); d) Base of Spanish column (photo by author); e) Relief panel fragment (drawing by author after Matos Moctezuma 1997:f.7); f) Recarved millstone (photo by author).

Part II: The Importance of Tlaltecuhtli in Aztec Worldview

Before one presents a detailed analysis of Tlaltecuhtli 1 and 2 iconography, it is important to first outline and describe the deity's role in Aztec history, myth, and ritual. In other words, a description of Tlaltecuhtli's role in Aztec belief creates a background upon which the details of earth iconography can be laid and thereby given context and meaning. First in importance is Tlaltecuhtli's dual personality, the belief in the earth as both ally and enemy, producer and consumer, source of nourishment and force of destruction. One sees this duality expressed especially in the form of Tlaltecuhtli 1, the female earth, marked as a site of both creation and of death. Second, it is important to emphasize that Tlaltecuhtli, far from being a secondary deity, in fact played as important a role as the sun in Aztec belief and ritual practice. That the earth was considered key not only in Aztec religion, but the organization of the Aztec Empire, is indicated by the Templo Mayor itself, which appears to have been viewed as a physical manifestation of Tlaltecuhtli. It also appears that the Templo Mayor, great symbol of the Aztecs and the Aztec State, utilized a triadic arrangement of water, sun, and earth (twin temples and their temple platform) alongside the more generally acknowledged duality of Tlaloc and Huitzilopochtli.

Dismemberment and Rebirth: Sacrifice and Reciprocity

Tlaltecuhtli's personality was one of fundamental duality, combining themes of life and production with death and consumption. The Aztecs believed that the earth was alive, a conscious, coherent being with the ability to both create and destroy, nourish and starve. This ambivalent temperament towards mankind is a direct result of the earth's creation, a myth retold in the *Histoire du Mechique* (Garibay 1973) in which the earth is depicted as a great, primordial victim of sacrifice who, as a result of her abuses, cries out for human blood as a means of compensation.

In the *Histoire du Mechique*, the earth begins as a great monster walking upon the primordial sea (Garibay 1973:108). Tezcatlipoca and Quetzalcoatl, taking the form of two snakes, set upon this creature and tear it limb from limb. The gods then use half of Tlaltecuhtli's body to create the earth while the other half is taken up to become the sky. The other gods, appalled at this violent dismemberment of the earth, "...descended to console her[6] and commanded that all the fruits necessary for the life of mankind generate from her" (Ibid.). From this moment, all living things sprout from Tlaltecuhtli's body, trees and grass from the deity's hair and skin, caves and lakes from the deity's eyes. Despite such hearty reparation from the gods, however, "This goddess at times cried out in the night, yearning to eat the hearts of men, and she would not quiet herself as long as they were not given to her, nor would she give fruit unless quenched with the blood of men" (Ibid.). As Taube states, "As a result, humans had to nourish Tlaltecuhtli with their own hearts and blood to placate the violated earth" (2004:170).

This mythic dismemberment of the earth is seen in several contexts related to earth goddesses and may have been reenacted at the Ochpaniztli rites, ceremonies devoted to the Aztec earth goddess, Teteo Innan. In these rites, victims were dismembered by being pushed off of poles standing 180 feet high (this may be an exaggeration on the part of Durán). Durán describes the victim's death: "He fell from the poles with a mighty crash and was shattered to bits" (1971:234). After this fall, the victims were beheaded. Their blood was caught in a bowl from which the priest drank, an act that caused the earth to quake (Ibid:235).

This type of sacrifice by dismemberment also recalls the death of Coyolxauhqui, albeit in reverse order, in which Coyolxauhqui was decapitated by Huitzilopochtli and thrown down the side of Coatepec. An early depiction of the dismembered Coyolxauhqui (the predecessor of the famous Coyolxauhqui stone), still in situ at the base of the Templo Mayor, presents the goddess with her detached limbs aligned to the four cardinal directions. As Taube states, "Coyolxauhqui is rendered as the earth, dismembered and fashioned into a new, ordered world... from the dismembered Coyolxauhqui and the bodies of vanquished enemies, the Aztec world was made" (2004:174). Therefore, the dismemberment and decapitation of sacrifices during Ochpaniztli as well as that of Coyolxauhqui at the hill of Coatepec, may reference the first act of cosmic creation in which the body of the earth was torn apart to create the world of humankind.

For Graulich, the Tlaltecuhtli creation myth "...explain[s] the origin of the earth, heaven—or a part of it—and of plants, but also the need for human sacrifice and, in all probability, for death" (1997:51; see also Graulich 1988:576). Matos Moctezuma also discusses this dismemberment of the earth goddess as a preliminary step of world creation and production:

> The story of *Tlaltecuhtli*, 'earth lord,'... dramatizes how the creation of the earth was formed from a coherent bodily structure... while the landscape was conceived as a corporeal entity—a living being—it was the destruction or reformation of that being that was required to promote a wider spectrum of life. Life, in the Aztec cosmogony, was not composed of a unified body but rather as a result of the violent

[6] All gendered references by quoted authors have been left unchanged.

actions of destruction; of tearing a body apart to create new combinations of matter sustaining a plurality of beings. (1995:39)

In many ways, the myth of the earth's creation is the model for the Aztec view of their world—the mutual dependence of life and death and the inextricable connection between human sacrifice and the survival of humankind.

Throughout the Americas, cultures perceive of dismemberment as a creative force. Gillespie, for instance, points out that "...the Mesoamerican worldview shared in the nearly universal theme of dismemberment as a source of primordial creation and fertility" (1991:333-334). The earth, however, was a duality, in which creativity and productivity were juxtaposed against powers of death and destruction. As Seler states, "The earth is an animal that, on the one hand, carries trees and plants on its broad back and allows the corn plants to grow... on the other hand, it is a monster that sucks up the water that drips from the heavens, that swallows into its belly the bones of the dead and the sun as its [sic] descends in the evening, and even the souls of the deceased" (1990-[V]:5).

Many authors focus on the darker aspects of the earth. Nuttall, for instance, states: "It is obvious how the constant associations of the earth-mother with sanguinary sacrifices and bloodthirstiness would, in time, give rise to the idea of a hostile, maleficent power, linked with darkness and devouring fire..." (1901:66). Brundage paints an equally sinister picture: "...the earth, was pitiless and inhuman; she stood in a sense beyond effective petition. Her will was to bring men, beasts and all growing things out of her womb, to make them feel her hollow and echoing power... to feed them, to frighten them, and then to call them, lurching and falling, back into the heart of her darkness" (1972:96). In a later article Brundage describes the impact of the earth on the Aztecs as "...a religious seizure and a terror which had nothing intellectual about it" (1979:154).

Discussions of Tlaltecuhtli as a hostile and chaotic force may cause an emphasis on the darker aspects of Tlaltecuhtli imagery over all else as a visual expression of Aztec terror and fear. Descriptions of the earth as chaos incarnate— "Tlalteotl[7] is a savage beast; she is chaos..." (Graulich 1997:51; see also Graulich 1988:576 and Pasztory 1983:82)—may also lead one to assume that representations of the earth might be similarly disorganized and arbitrary. Instead, representations of Tlaltecuhtli are extremely structured, the exchange of elements governed by strict rules and, especially in Tlaltecuhtli 2, an almost obsessive attention to consistency. Perhaps this contrast between the chaotic Tlaltecuhtli of myth and the controlled nature of the deity's iconography may best be understood as a reflection of the earth's transition from a confused primordial form to its current ordered state. Through the deity's violent dismemberment, chaos was transformed into the coherent patterns of life.

Sun and Earth: Tlaltecuhtli's Role in Aztec Ritual

Despite the fact that the sun and earth are often paired in sixteenth-century sources, contemporary scholarship has often focused on the singular role of the sun in the lives of the Aztecs (Graulich 1988:396). It is clear, however, that the earth played just as vital a role in Aztec worldview. In myth and ritual, the earth and sun were held in equal regard, for the universe was considered to be equally reliant on both for its continued existence. This pairing reflects the fundamental principle of duality with which the Aztecs viewed their world, a duality in which opposite forces were considered two halves of a whole, equally necessary and mutually dependent (López Austín 1988:52-53, 57; 1990:160,167-179). Female agrarian connections of the rainy season were contrasted against the male dry season pastimes of warfare and hunting (Klein 1976:33; Matos Moctezuma 1991:22) and were further echoed in the division of night from day (Graulich 1997:129-131).

Even the foundation myth of Tenochtitlan is replete with joint references to the sun and earth. A solar heart falls upon a terrestrial stone and a cactus is born (Durán 1994:41, 32-33, 42). That an eagle, avatar of the sun, makes his home within this cactus, a plant which sprouts from the earth, echoes the joining of the heart and stone. The duality of earth and sun were further reflected in the political organization of the Aztec state in which the *Tlatoani*, associated with Huitzilopochtli, the sun, and masculinity, was paired with an advisor called *Cihuacoatl*, a position linked to the earth and women (see López Austín 1988:76, 1990:169; Nuttall 1901:62). The joining of such oppositions was believed to form the basic framework of the cosmos and their delicate balance was considered key to the continued functioning of the universe.

The role that the earth played *vis à vis* the sun is also wrapped up in oppositions. On the one hand, the earth was the greatest enemy of the sun, consuming him at dusk into the dark Underworld where he would have to undergo great battles to be reborn. Imagery of the figure Tlalchitonatiuh is a particularly vivid illustration of this consumption of the sun by the earth (see Thompson 1943; Taube 1998; Krickeberg 1961; Alcina Franch 1995). Tlalchitonatiuh (Figure 8) is a composite deity comprised of a dark-skinned Tonatiuh or mummy-bundle Tonatiuh wearing a Tlaloc mask who sinks into the open jaws of Tlaltecuhtli 1a. Though at times this figure is described as portraying the sun's emergence from the earth (Thompson 1943:120), the imagery appears more

[7] "Tlalteotl" means "earth deity" and is equivalent to "Tlaltecuhlti," though used far less frequently. As Seler states, "Tlaltecutli, not *tlalteotl* is the standard expression for the divinity of the earth" (1990-[III]:249).

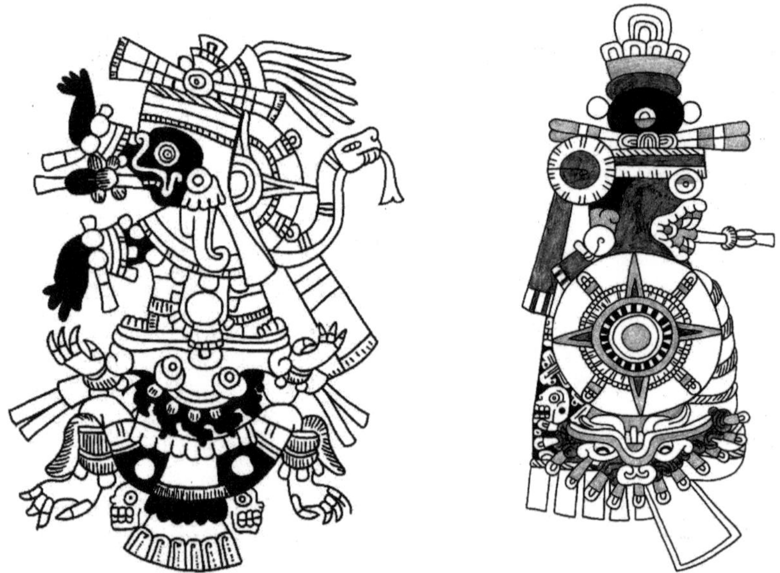

Figure 8: Deity Variant Tlalchitonatiuh: a) Codex Telleriano Remensis (drawing by author after Quiñones Keber 1995:20r); b) Codex Borbonicus (drawing by author after Seler 1963[II]:f.270).

closely associated with solar descent and death, particularly when Tonatiuh is shown as a mummy bundle (Figure 8b; see also the Codex Aubin image (Seler 1963[I]:f.376)). As Seler describes in the case of the Borbonicus image, "…the sun sinking into the jaws of the earth is pictured as a bundled corpse, a sun corpse…" (1990-[V]:5). Furthermore, Durán refers to the name Tlalchitonatiuh as "setting sun" (1994:296).

This relationship between the earth and sun was not simply one of consumer and consumed, however. The sun was also considered the child of the earth, emerging every morning from her womb at dawn. In fact, contemporary Huichol see all births as analogous to the birth of the sun: "When a woman gives birth, they say she is giving light, like the rays of the sun. Every time a child is born it is like the sun rising to complete another day" (Schaefer 1989:191). The mother-child relationship between the earth and sun is illustrated by the mythic birth of Huitzilopochtli (a solar deity) from Coatlicue (an earth goddess) at Coatepec. Huitzilopochtli's battle against, decapitation, and dismemberment of Coyolxauhqui, an earth goddess, however, demonstrate that the sun and earth were also considered enemies.

One might wonder how the earth can simultaneously be the mother and the enemy of the sun, but it must be remembered that the Aztecs conceived of the mother-child relationship as one of conflict. A woman undertook childbirth as a warrior entering the battlefield: "Seize well thy little shield. My daughter, my youngest one, be thou a brave woman; face it—that is, bear down; imitate the brave woman Cihuacoatl, Quilaztli" (Sahagún 1950-82[VI]:160). This parental bond is also seen in the metaphorical allusion to captives as the sons of their captors (Sahagún 1950-82[II]:52-53). Both in battle and in childbirth, the relationship between children and their parents was envisioned as one of antagonism. It is thus easy to see how the earth could have, at once, given birth to as well as battled against the sun.

That the importance of Tlaltecuhtli has so often been overlooked is not surprising, given the fact that references to the deity in sixteenth-century documents are frequently couched in the poetics of the Nahuatl language. In Sahagún, for instance, it often appears that Tlaltecuhtli *is* the sun: "May the eagle warrior, the ocelot warrior, endure, live—he who is the gladdener, the servant of the sun. Somewhere, sometime, thou wilt grant that they will follow the sun, Tlaltecuhtli" (1950-82[VI]:15). Rather than a conflation of Tlaltecuhtli with the sun, however, this phrasing instead juxtaposes the sun and earth in the Aztec tradition of *difrasismo*, "…a process in which a single idea is expressed through two words that complete its meaning, either by being synonyms or by being adjacent" (Garibay 1970:115). In this case, following the sun and Tlaltecuhtli refers to the impending death of warriors, whose bodies will be swallowed by Tlaltecuhtli and whose souls will go to accompany the sun to its zenith. The same analogy is made in the description of a warrior as "…the noble one who will attain the lap, the bosom of the sun, Tlaltecuhtli" (Ibid.:11).

The sun is often portrayed in contemporary literature as the sole receiver of human sacrifice, though sixteenth-century sources almost always pair the sun and the earth as dual consumers of such offerings. For instance, according to Durán, before their sacrifice by the Aztecs, a group of captured Huastec warriors were called "Children of the Sun" and "Children of the Lord of the Earth"

(1994:167; see also Tezozomoc 1987:626). In the *Leyenda de los Soles,* the pairing of the sun and earth is also referenced in a tale in which the sun tells Mixcoatl and his four companions to kill the four hundred Mimixcoa warriors "...in order to nourish him and Tlaltecuhtli for they were, he added, father and mother of mankind. These 400 who were exterminated became the prototypes of the prisoners of war to be sacrificed..." (Graulich 1988:395). In this story, explicit reference is made not only to the sun and the earth as dual creators of mankind, but also to the fact that human sacrifice was intended to feed *both* the sun *and* the earth. This may explain why *cuauhxicalli,* "eagle vessels" are decorated with both sun and earth imagery, as they were considered joint consumers of such sacrifices (Graulich 1988:398).

It is clear, then, that the purpose of war was as much to feed the earth as it was to provide the sun with blood. This role is emphasized throughout Sahagún. A midwife's words to a newborn male child, for instance, were: "[Y]our office and your purpose is war; your destiny is to give drink to the sun with the blood of the enemies and to feed the earth, called 'Tlaltecuhtli,' with the bodies of your enemies" (Matos Moctezuma 1995:27-28, citing Sahagún 1956). Warriors were similarly described, "...they have been dedicated [on earth], there promised, born at this time, sent to such a place to provide drink, to provide food, to provide offerings for the sun, for the lord of the earth" (1950-82[VI]:12).

Graulich (1988) emphasizes the importance of double immolations as necessary in feeding both the sun and the earth. Though the majority of sacrifices recorded in sixteenth-century sources are described as performed by heart extraction, decapitation was another popular form of sacrifice. In Durán, for instance, priests are said to have told their victims that they were there "...to offer your chests and your throats to the knife" (1994:157), thereby referencing both heart sacrifice and decapitation. In general, however, the sixteenth-century accounts often gloss over the rite of decapitation, a rite that may have accompanied most sacrifices (Brundage 1979:212).[8] Therefore, though Durán never mentions decapitation in his lengthy description of the rituals that accompanied the dedication of the Templo Mayor, his statement that the old *tzompantli* was destroyed and a new one was erected for the numerous new sacrificial victims (1994:341) should be seen as an indication of the importance of decapitation in these dedication rites. The statement of the conquistador Andrés de Tapia that the *tzompantli* in the central precinct of Tenochtitlan held 136,000 heads (Baquedano and Graulich 1993:164) similarly indicates the commonality and importance of decapitation, even when the distinct probability of exaggeration is taken into account. It is also important to recall how predominantly decapitation appears in accounts of Aztec rituals, especially in relation to ceremonies in honor of female, earth-related deities (Klein 1988:243; Joyce 2000:166).

Graulich discusses the reason why the Aztecs dedicated hearts to the sun and heads to the earth: "The fact that the ritual immolation by excision of the heart was directed more in particular to the sun was quite logical since the heart symbolized and indeed *was* the movement the sun needed to keep going. It was a sacrifice to heavenly fire and to carry it out only a flint knife could be used, for flint was or contained a spark descended from heaven" (1988:401). For the Aztecs, the human heart was seen as the seat of movement and heat, and therefore their dedication to the sun was considered appropriate. "Decapitation, on the other hand generated streams of blood that drenched the earth so that she 'would bear fruit', as promised in the creation myths" (Baquedano and Graulich 1993:165; see also Graulich 1988:394). Blood, like water, was needed to fertilize the earth, and therefore decapitation, on the one hand echoing the initial dismemberment of the earth in creation myths, on the other hand served the very practical purpose of soaking the earth with blood. These double immolations may also be related to the fact that a person's two most vital life forces, the *teyolia* and the *tonalli,* were located in the heart and head, respectively (López Austín 1988:204; Carrasco 1990:68-70).

Dualities and Triads: Tlaltecuhtli and the Templo Mayor

The great site where these double immolations took place, the Templo Mayor, also has direct ties to Tlaltecuhtli. For instance, the temple itself bore the same mixed associations as the earth. "[O]n the mythological level Templo Mayor, the sacred mountain, was the earth itself, the earth as a voracious monster devouring human victims and blood. At the same time, the earth contained regenerative forces that linked it to agricultural growth and fertility in general" (Broda 1987:105). As Arnold describes, "The Templo Mayor was the site of an enormous earth opening. In particular it was the mouth of the earth lord, Tlaltecuhtli, who would receive nourishment through blood sacrifices" (1999:53). The reward for such sacrifices was continued agricultural growth and production.

Graulich provides an interesting description of the double immolations that took place at the Templo Mayor: "...the action consisting in beheading the victim and throwing it down to the earth was inversely symmetrical to the extraction of the heart and its elevation toward the sun. The terrace at the base of the pyramid where the body was to fall was called the 'banquet table,' in other words, the place where Tlaltecuhtli ate" (1988:402). The Coyolxauhqui stone (Figure 10b), which once lay at the base of the pyramid, shows the goddess as a great victim

[8] Such dual sacrifices also appear to have occurred in the Maya area: "...it is well to bear in mind that decapitation at times followed removal of the heart" (Thompson 1970:179). As Robicsek and Hales state, the iconography of Maya ceramic vases "...suggests that heart sacrifice was connected to, and probably practiced together with, ritual decapitation" (1984:50).

of sacrifice, beheaded and dismembered by Huitzilopochtli. This figure, however, also shows striking iconographic parallels to the earth, including masked joints, skulls tied on to the elbows and knees, a skull-topped back apron, wristlets, and anklets edged with bells. Here, then, it seems that Coyolxauhqui is represented both as a sacrifice and as the earth, receiver of such sacrifices (see Broda 1987). The platform of the Templo Mayor should thus be understood as a great receptacle of blood and bodies, the "banquet table" of Tlaltecuhtli and symbol of the earth itself.

With its twin temples to Tlaloc and Huitzilopochtli, the Templo Mayor obviously represented themes of duality—night and day, rainy season and dry season, agriculture and war (López Luján 1994 96; Matos Moctezuma 1984:133). The Aztecs, however, structured their universe in multiple ways, simultaneously employing dual, triple, and even quadripartite schemes (see Van Zantwijk 1985:22). The Aztecs thus utilized a triadic model of earth, sky, and Underworld, as well as one of water, sun, and earth alongside their more often cited framework of dual oppositions. Tezozomoc illustrates the latter triad by describing war captives as "...the sons of the Lord of the earth *Tlacteuctli*, sons of the Sun, and sons of the God of water" (1987:626). The Templo Mayor, then, was not only a dual structure, but simultaneously represented a triad. As Matos Moctezuma states, "...the Templo possessed three elements necessary for life: earth (the terrestrial level of the Templo and of Coatlicue), water (Tlaloc), and the sun (Huitzilopochtli)" (1995:72).

Further evidence for the Templo Mayor as a temple to these three deities comes from Díaz del Castillo, who describes the temple as containing three idols, including Huitzilopochtli and Tezcatlipoca , though the description of this latter deity, who had "a countenance like a bear, and great shining eyes" indicates that he was probably a fanged and goggled Tlaloc instead (1927[I]:179). The third deity is described as follows: "...we saw a figure half human and the other half resembling an alligator... This idol was said to contain the germ, and origin of all created things, and was the god of harvest, and fruits" (Ibid.). This final deity, then, is most likely a representation of Tlaltecuhtli, the fecund earth who contained the seed of all living things. The Templo Mayor may therefore be understood as embracing two different numerical models by which the Aztecs organized their cosmos. On the one hand it was a duality, joining the images and associations of Tlaloc and Huitzilopochtli. On another, perhaps deeper, level, however, the Templo Mayor represented a triad, the co-dependence of the aquatic Tlaloc and the solar Huitzilopochtli upon the terrestrial Tlaltecuhtli.[9]

[9] A massive stone slab carved with the image of a dorsal Tlaltecuhtli 1 figure has recently been discovered at the base of the Templo Mayor. This massive sculpture, which measures some four meters long and weighs about twelve metric tons, appears to support the arguments given above. At the current time (Fall 2006), excavations, directed by A. Barrerra (Programa de Arqueología Urbana del INAH), are in progress and have not yet uncovered the entire surface of the monolith. (I am grateful to Leonardo López Luján for pointing out this new discovery, pers. comm. 2006)

Part III: Tlaltecuhtli Iconography

A General Outline of Tlaltecuhtli Imagery

As was discussed in the introduction, the three universal features shared by all Tlaltecuhtli images are that they are two-dimensional, depicted in a straight-on view, and represent the deity in the splayed hocker body position. The first of these may be seen as somewhat determined by media, for Tlaltecuhtli imagery is, for the most part, limited to codex depictions and bas-relief carvings in stone. It is interesting, however, in light of the predominance of Tlaltecuhtli imagery in stone, that the deity was never depicted in three dimensions or in-the-round as so many other sculptures of Aztec deities are.[10] As a result, it appears that the flattening of Tlaltecuhtli into two dimensions was a conscious and significant decision.

The second requirement of Tlaltecuhtli images is that they must be depicted in a straight-on view. Klein addresses the meaning behind *en face* imagery by discussing "...the relation of frontality to the themes of death, darkness, earth, and descent..." (1976:15). *En face* images often appear to have been associated with such themes by their positioning on objects. "Two-dimensional frontal images in Mesoamerica appear in visual contexts that often locate their subject matter in cosmological space" (Ibid.:176, 177). Therefore, images of Tlaltecuhtli, the terrestrial deity *par excellence*, were positioned beneath objects, the deity both taking on the position of the earth as well as resting against the earth itself.

Klein also remarks upon the way in which *en face* imagery engages the viewer (1976:19-20). She discusses the powerful reaction that results from such a pose as a result of its emphasis on the central axis of the human body:

> This impression of direct confrontation is reinforced by the fact that the heart, the navel, and the sex organs appear on the vertical axis of a frontal figure; the viewer's attention is immediately drawn to these centrally-located body parts. Thus the frontal figure, unlike the profile figure, automatically attracts the viewer's attention to several of the most vital organs of the body. (Ibid.:42)

Several of these arguments also hold true for dorsal images of Tlaltecuhtli, which similarly emphasize the vertical axis and symmetry of the human body. Tlaltecuhtli, always depicted in a straight-on view, then, is not only associated with themes of darkness, earth, and death, but also with power, direct engagement, and intense confrontation.

The final diagnostic feature of Tlaltecuhtli, and the one that deserves the most attention due to its many conflicting interpretations, is the deity's body position—outstretched arms bent up at the elbows, legs splayed, and knees bent. Though Tlaltecuhtli is by no means the only deity shown in this hocker pose, it is one of Tlaltecuhtli's most diagnostic features. Consequently, when other gods are presented in such a position, it is usually a means of linking them to aspects of the earth. The five possible interpretations of this pose are that it represents the world directions, parturition, defeat, descent, or a saurian or amphibian identity.

The first of these, directionality, is never mentioned in contemporary scholarship, perhaps because the conflation of the body of the earth with the quadripartite universe seems self-evident. The hocker position, however, does appear to have had a directional meaning, representing the splayed human body as symbol of the four world quarters. Nuttall, for instance, discusses the human body, especially the sacrificial victim when stretched out over the sacrificial stone, as a metaphor for the world directions (1901:174, 91-92), while Carrasco calls the human body "a living, moving center of the world" (1990:21, 52-54). León-Portilla speaks similarly of the Aztec conception of their earth: "...the universe is divided into four great quadrants of space whose common point of departure is the navel of the earth." (1963:57). Such metaphors are also seen in the Maya area, where sacrificial victims were tied to crosses, symbols of the quadripartite world (see Thompson 1970:176-178). It is important to note that Tlaltecuhtli is never identified in the codices with a specific direction (Klein 1976:56), so it is quite possible that the deity's body was considered all directions at once, the navel marking the world center. The hocker position may therefore have reflected the earth's quadripartite division, a simple correlation between the body of Tlaltecuhtli and the quarters of the earth. That the outspread body of the earth was symbolic of the four directions is also seen in ballgame imagery, where the four-quartered ballcourt and the body of the earth are at times conflated (Figure 30a).

The most popular explanation for the hocker position is that it represents birth, the squatting *mamazouhticac* position of native women (Klein 1973; Nicholson 1954; Gutiérrez Solana 1983; Matos Moctezuma 1997). The primary evidence supporting the hocker position as one of parturition is that deities found in this pose are often seen with creation imagery: new figures emerging from them in representations of birth. The most vivid image in support of the hocker position as a birth pose is found in

[10] Because of its crossed-legged pose and the wearing of a loincloth, I do not consider the three-dimensional "Coatlique del Metro" a pure Tlaltecuhtli image, but rather some kind of deity variant.

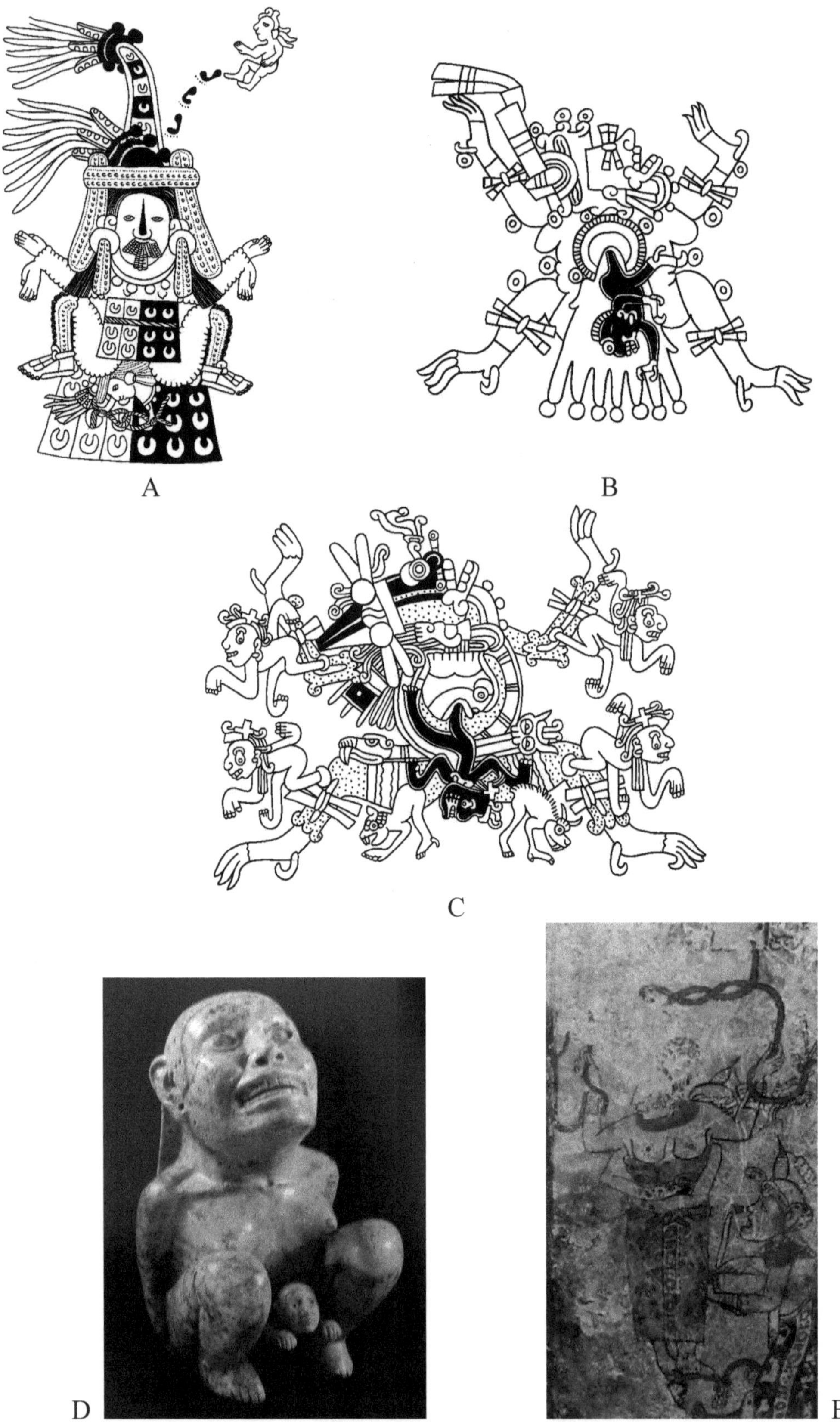

Figure 9: Birth Imagery: a) Birth scene of Tlazolteotl (drawing by author after Seler 1963[I]:f.347); b) Birth scene from Borgia (drawing by author after Díaz and Rodgers 1993:pl.31); c) Nanahuatzin Born out of the Joints of a Skeletal God (drawing by author after Díaz and Rodgers 1993:pl.42); d) Greenstone Tlazolteotl giving birth (Matos Moctezuma and Solís 2002:f.320); e) Maya Birth Vase showing woman giving birth while holding on to ropes from rafters (Rollout © Justin Kerr, K5113).

the Codex Borbonicus (Figure 9a) in which a small figure emerges from a squatting Tlazolteotl. A number of other images depicting the hocker position as one of birth can also be found in the Borgia Codex. In one instance, a human figure emerges in a gush of blood from the abdomen of a blindfolded goddess (Figure 9b). In another, figures that appear to be Nanahuatzin sprout from the joints of a squatting male deity (Figure 9c). A number of these images depict birth as emergence from the abdomen rather than the womb, indicating that the stomach, the center of the body – marked at birth as the terminus of the umbilical cord—was considered as much the locale of creation and birth as the womb, vagina, or birth canal.

Importantly, however, there are also instances where explicit birth scenes do not show the mother in the hocker position. First among these is the greenstone image identified as Tlazolteotl giving birth (Figure 9d). In this graphic portrayal of parturition, a human figure emerges from the vagina of the goddess, while Tlazolteotl's clenched teeth and anguished expression emphasize the realism of the image. Notably, however, neither Tlazolteotl's arms or legs are splayed. Quezada records the squatting pose of this statuette as a conventional birth position, "The position for birth was crouching down with the hands on the buttocks, with the fingers partially opening the vulva" (1977:314). In another image, found on the "Birth Vase" from the Maya area, a woman gives birth while holding onto a rope slung from the rafters (see Taube 1994) (Figure 9e). This birth position is known ethnographically and is discussed by Guiteras-Holmes (1961:107). Again, though the arms here are similar to the hocker position, the legs are straight. Though both the greenstone statuette and the Maya vase indicate that caution should be used when equating the hocker position unequivocally with birth, however, they by no means disprove such a theory. The fact that two of the most explicit representations of birth known from Mesoamerica are so different from one another leads one to instead conclude that there may have been a variety of poses used by women in childbirth, the hocker among them.

In the case of true Tlaltecuhtli imagery—rather than imagery of other deities taking on her body position—only one instance inarguably depicts birth or creation. This image shows Tezcatlipoca emerging from a *chalchihuitl* sign on the abdomen of Tlaltecuhtli (Figure 2b). Though this portrayal of the birth of Tezcatlipoca is more metaphorical than realistic, it nonetheless clearly depicts emergence from the earth's center. As for other Tlaltecuhtli images, none show the physical result of birth. The reason for this may be quite simple: in most Tlaltecuhtli 1 relief images—the female version of the earth most likely to be involved in birth scenes—the viewer is presented with Tlaltecuhtli's back. That she is depicted in a dorsal view is made clear by the presence of a skull ornament, other examples of which are found on the "Coatlicue del Metro" (Matos Moctezuma and Solís 2002:f.132), the colossal Coatlicue statue (Figure 10a), the Coyolxauhqui Stone (Figure 10b), and throughout the codices as a back ornament worn by female deities (Figure 10c). This skull thus marks the greater part of Tlaltecuhtli 1 figures as facing away from the viewer. As birth is generally represented taking place through the navel, such events would occur on the face opposite that available to the viewer.

Klein (1988) has presented an interesting alternative to the traditional birth theory. Rather than showing parturition, Klein argues, the hocker position presents us with a defeated enemy. Likening the splayed pose of the earth deity to the pelts of animals taken in the hunt, Klein theorizes that Tlaltecuhtli imagery represents a defeated woman warrior, subjugated and humiliated by the male state. Klein (1994), for instance, discusses Tlaltecuhtli as conceptually equivalent to Cihuacoatl, the first defeated enemy of Huitzilopochtli. It is important to mention, however, that arguments about female subjugation only relate to Tlaltecuhtli 1, for Tlaltecuhtli 2 is fully male. Regardless, however, the similarity of Tlaltecuhtli's pose to those of skins portrayed in such codices as the Magliabechiano cannot be overlooked (Figure 11a). A vivid representation of the flaying of a sacrificial victim in the Primeros Memoriales (Figure 11b) further supports this association of the hocker position with defeat and sacrifice.

The strongest iconographic support for the argument that the hocker position represents defeat is found in the Teocalli of Moctezuma (Figure 1b), where the image of Tlaltecuhtli is shown face down on the throne's seat. The ruler would, literally, have been seated upon the back of the earth. Though the sun symbol carved into the seat back also alludes to the positioning of the ruler between earth and sky, images of flayed animal skins (Figure 11c) and defeated enemies sat upon and stood upon by rulers throughout Mesoamerica link such a position to that of military defeat as well (see also Carrera 1979:190; Townsend 1979:55; Umberger 1981:190). One should also consider the description of the earth's creation from the *Histoire du Mechique*, which situates Tlaltecuhtli as a sacrificial victim, set upon and torn in two by Tezcatlipoca and Quetzalcoatl (Garibay 1973).

In the case of Tlaltecuhtli 1 imagery, however—the female variant of the earth that would have best embodied concepts of the defeated enemy of the Aztec state—the Teocalli of Moctezuma (Figure 1b), the base of the Bilimek vessel (Figure 2a), and possibly the base of the Stuttgart statuette (Figure 5d) are the only representations of Tlaltecuhtli 1 known to show the goddess facing the ground. Though dorsal images of Tlaltecuhtli 1 are common, they are often carved underneath *cuauhxicalli* vessels, figures, and offertory boxes. In these cases, therefore, when placed in situ, Tlaltecuhtli actually faced upwards, with her back upon the ground. As a result,

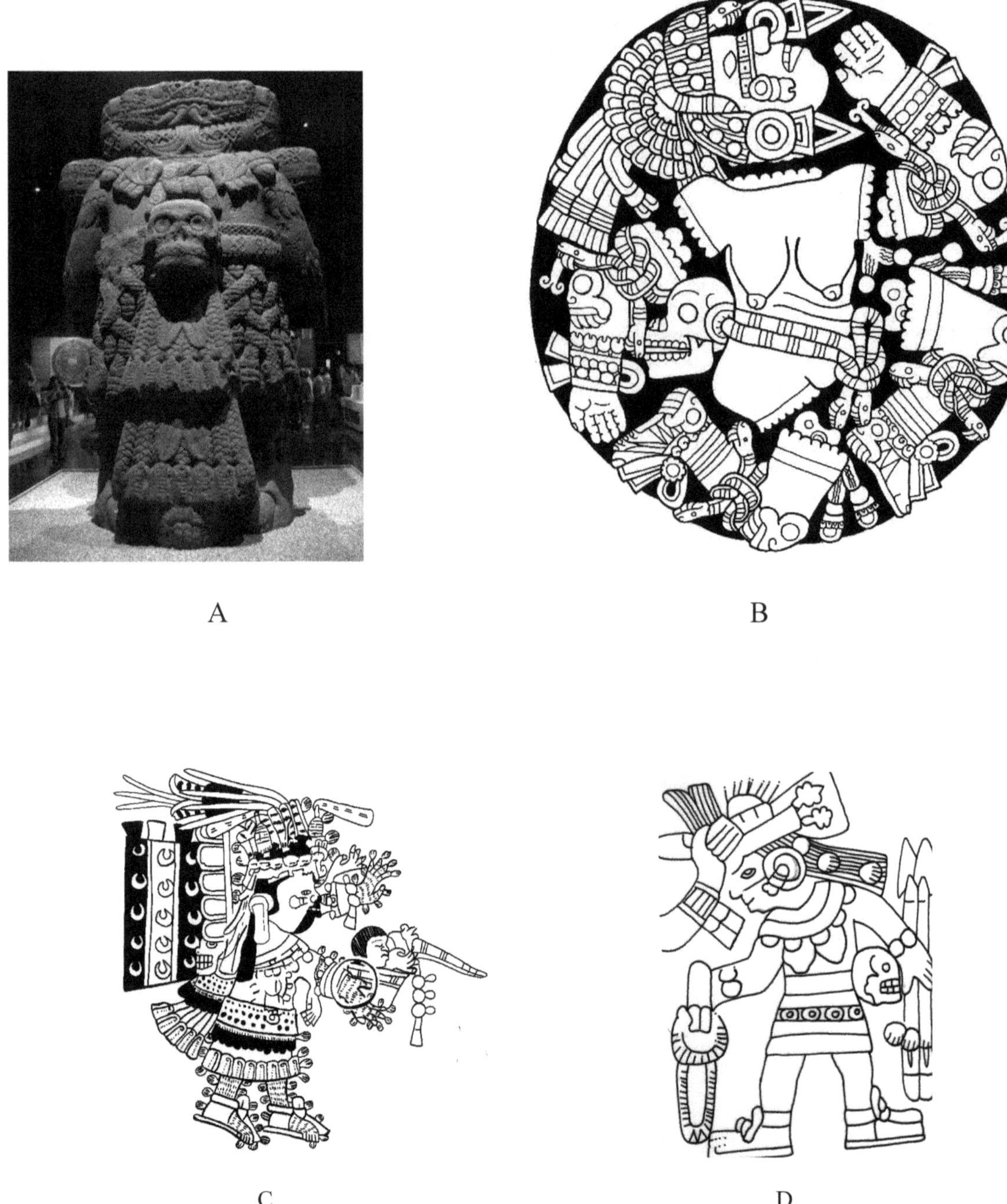

Figure 10: Back Skulls: a) Colossal "Coatlicue" (photo by author); b) Coyolxauhqui Stone (Taube 1993:49); c) Ixcuina (Telleriano Remensis 17v) (drawing by author after Quiñones Keber 1995:f.17v); d) Stone of Moctezuma (drawing by author after Alcina Franch, et al. 1992:f.XLI)

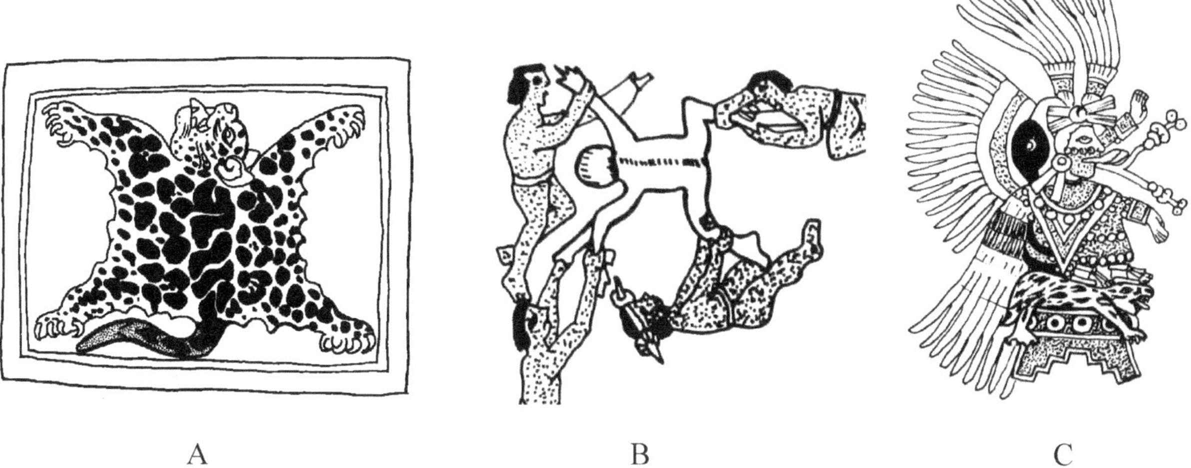

Figure 11: Images of Skins and Sacrifice: a) Codex Magliabechiano (drawing by author after Boone 1983); b) Primeros Memoriales (Klein 1988:f.11a); c) Xochiquetzal seated on skin (Ibid.:f.10b).

objects generally would not have been placed on Tlaltecuhtli's back as a sign of her defeat, but instead were conceptually located on her abdomen, previously discussed as a site of birth. In Mesoamerican art, animal pelts are never shown face-up, and though some defeated warriors are depicted lying supine, these are never shown in the hocker position. The defeat theory also does not address the various creation and birth scenes so often associated with the hocker position in the codices. If such a pose were always indicative of death and defeat, it seems the codices would not show it in so many contexts of creation.

Though Klein's theory may not be applicable to all Tlaltecuhtli imagery, it is important to remember that birth and death were considered very closely related in the minds of the Aztecs. As Seler notes, "The woman who gives birth is the warrior who takes a prisoner; the woman who dies in birth is the warrior who, fallen into the hands of his enemies, is sacrificed on the sacrificial stone" (1963[II]:181). This connection to war is seen not only on the seat of the Teocalli, where Tlaltecuhtli is shown bordered by two war shields (Figure 1b), but also in the Tlaltecuhtli image found on the sides of the "Stone of the Four Creations," where the goddess is flanked on either side by *atl tlachinolli* war signs (Figure 1e). The creation of the earth from the torn body of Tlaltecuhtli was an act of war undertaken by Quetzalcoatl and Tezcatlipoca, and the Aztecs believed creation and birth to come about via warfare and destruction. If one thinks of Tlaltecuhtli as having died in order to give birth to the world, as a mother dead in childbirth, then it is easy to see how she could simultaneously be shown in a position of parturition as well as of defeat and sacrifice.

A third interpretation of the hocker position is that it may depict descent. Rarely discussed by authors and dismissed as a possibility by Gutiérrez Solana (1983:24), it is nevertheless an intriguing theory in these contexts of birth and destruction and is clearly suggested iconographically in several instances. The first is a stone relief depiction of the body of Tlaltecuhtli—complete with mouths at her joints, clawed hands and feet, and the hocker body position—which bears the face and butterfly wings of Itzpapalotl (Figure 12a). Itzpapalotl, the "Obsidian Butterfly," is widely accepted to have been a *tzitzimitl*, a star demon who would descend at solar eclipses to wreak havoc on earth. As a result, this relief is frequently shown in illustrations with the head facing downwards (Klein 1976:59; Gutiérrez Solana 1983:f.177; Seler 1963[II]:f.267). Nothing, however, distinguishes the position of Itzpapalotl, here widely presumed to be descending headfirst to earth, from the hocker position of Tlaltecuhtli.

The second example of descent is a gold ornament identified by Solís (2004:162, f.71) as the head of Coyolxauhqui (Figure 12b). If one looks closely, however, one can discern a small body and limbs that show this goddess is in the splayed hocker position. As the ornament would have been worn with the face upright, it is clear that in this case, too, the hocker position is used to represent descent. Lastly, a sculpture of a Huastec goddess wearing a headdress of a monster descending in the hocker position (Figure 12c), not to mention the various descending gods from the sites of Tulum in Yucatan and El Tajín on the Gulf Coast, further indicate that such a pose was often associated with descent.

If, at the time of the earth's creation, one half of Tlaltecuhtli's body was thrown upwards to form the sky, it is conceivable that the deity would at times be shown descending like a *tzitzimitl*, bent on a venging its own

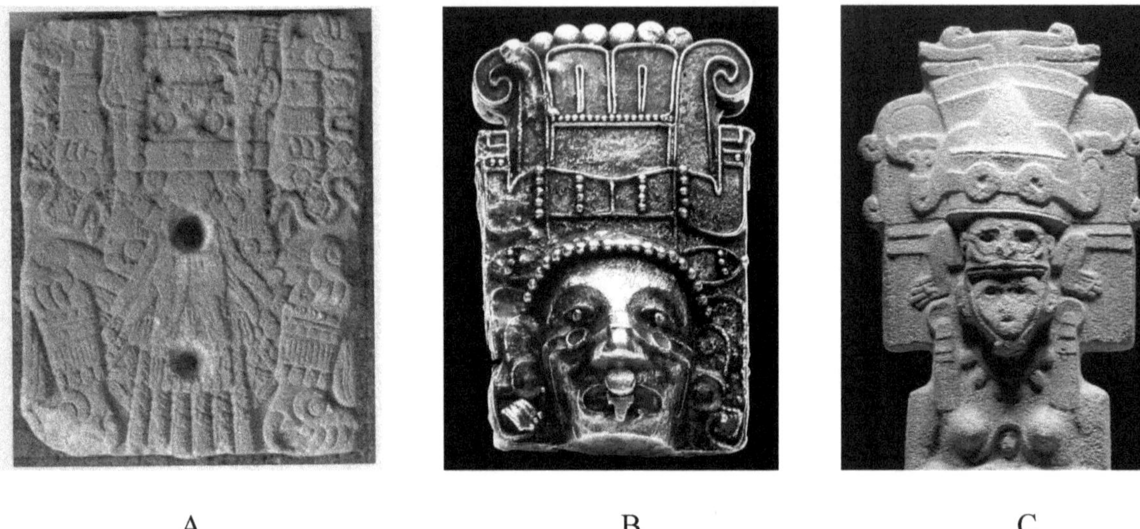

A B C

Figure 12: Descending Deities: a) Panel of Itzpapalotl (Boone 1999:f.17); b) Gold ornament with "Coyolxauhqui" face (Solís 2004:f.71); c) Huastec goddess with descending monster headdress (Ibid.f.178).

mistreatment by destroying mankind. As Klein states in a discussion of the *cihuateteo* and *tzitzimime,*[11] "All of the beings affiliated with the dark or terrestrial half of the cosmos were associated with the act of descent" (1976:33-34). This, of course, would include Tlaltecuhtli, the terrestrial deity *par excellence.* Descent, however, is not necessarily unequivocally associated with death and destruction. Klein, for instance, states that newborn babies were considered to have descended from the thirteenth heaven, an event possibly recorded in the Borbonicus 13 image where Tlazolteotl's child is seen descending to her from above (Klein 1976:35; see also León-Portilla 1963:118) (Figure 9a). Similarly, Seler calls Tamoanchan the "'Place of descent,' i.e. 'Place of birth'..." (1990-[V]:17). Descent was therefore associated with both the descent of the *tzitzimime* at the end of the world as well as the descent of children before birth.

Unfortunately, the only way to see whether Tlaltecuhtli images were once placed in a descending position is to discover relief panels in situ. Regrettably, however, there are very few Tlaltecuhtli images that have come from controlled excavations. In Baquedano and Orton's (1990) study, for instance, only four of the 37 sculptures discussed were discovered in their original context. Therefore, arguments based on the orientation of these images cannot, for the time being at least, be either proven or refuted.

The last concept associated with Tlaltecuhtli's hocker position is that it is linked to saurian, reptilian, or amphibian forms. Toads and frogs, conceived of as symbols of fertility and agricultural abundance throughout Mesoamerica, certainly carry similar associations as Tlaltecuhtli. As Klein states, "Frogs and toads are definitely connected with female sexuality in many parts of Mexico today" (1988:248). The primary textual evidence from early sources that supports such a connection comes from Mendieta, who describes Tlaltecuhtli as a giant toad with snapping mouths at every joint: "...the earth they took to be a goddess and they depicted her as a wild frog with mouths on all her joints filled with blood, saying that she ate and swallowed everything" (1945:87; see also Nicholson 1967:83; Klein 2000:11). Nicholson similarly describes Tlaltecuhtli as a "...toad-like creature studded with macabre symbols" (1972:225) and as a "...gigantic, crouching toadlike monster..." (1971:406). Three-dimensional sculptures of toads, when looked at from below, do have some iconographic similarity to deities shown in the hocker position (Nicholson 1967:83) (Figure 13a). Nicholson (Ibid.) specifically cites the *chalchihuitl* sign, framed by four jade beads, that is found on the abdomens of several toads as a symbol of the center, or heart, of the earth. This sign is found on the abdomens of at least three Tlaltecuhtli relief sculptures. Here, too, the symbol would refer to the center or womb of the earth.

According to Furst the concept of the earth as "...a monstrous toad with feline characteristics..." is quite widespread, possibly originating in South America (1972:37). The story of the South American Toad Grandmother, for instance, is remarkably similar to the

[11] These two groups of deities are difficult to differentiate. The main difference is that the *tzitzimime* (singular form "*tzitzimitl*") were envisioned as astral deities that threatened both the sun and mankind during eclipses. Klein (2000) does, however, discuss how the *tzitizmime* were demonized (and masculinized) after the Spanish Conquest, stripped of their ties to healing and curing to make them closer to the Christian concept of the devil (See Taube 1993b for discussion of the *tzitzimime* demons). The *cihuateteo* (singular form "*cihuateotl*"), on the other hand, whose identities often merge with the *tzitzimime*, were the souls of women who died in childbirth and, dressed as warriors, brought the sun from its zenith to its setting.

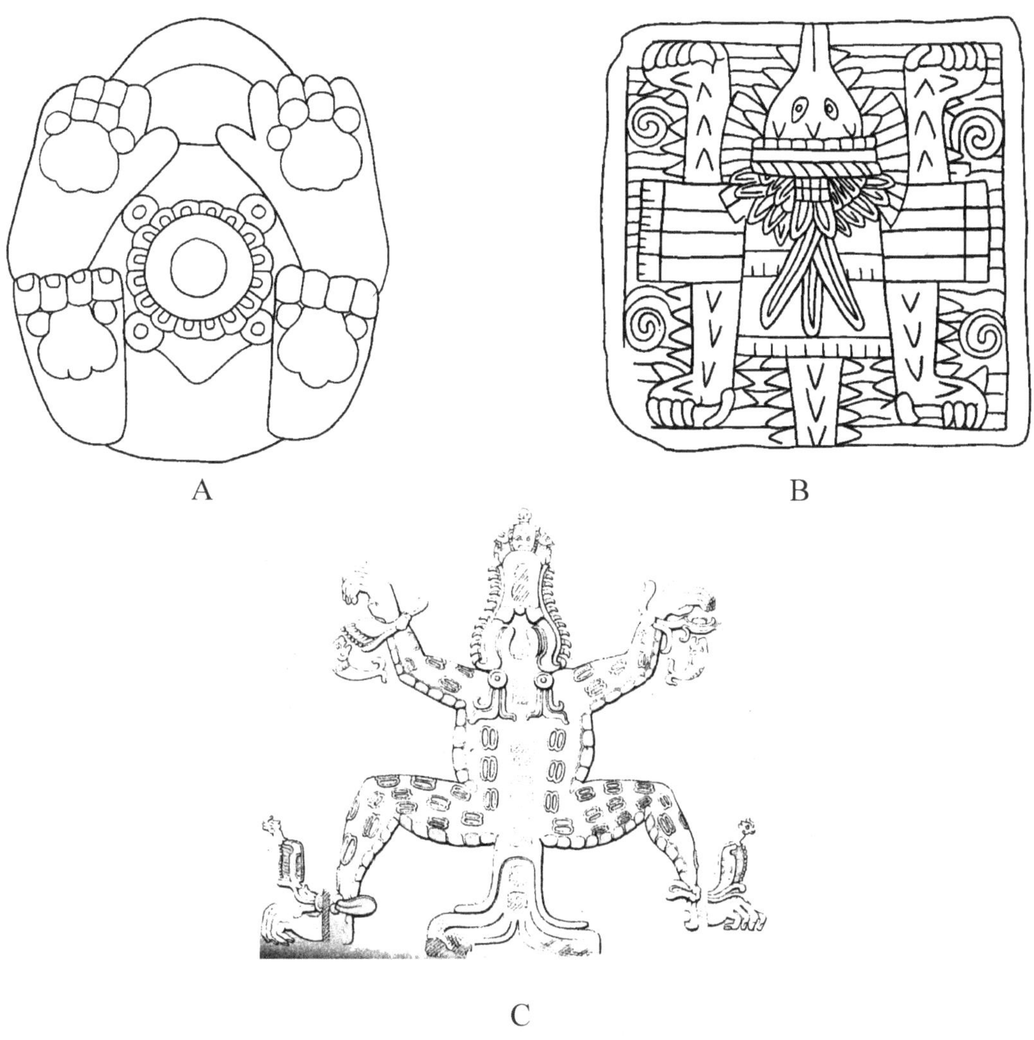

Figure 13: Saurian and Reptilian Imagery: a) Abdomen of a toad (drawing by author after Matos Moctezuma and Solís 2002:f.59); b) *Cipactli* (drawing by author after Gutiérrez Solana 1983:f.18, see also f.33); c) Splayed earth crocodile from Copan Altar T (Maudslay 1974).

creation myth of Tlaltecuhtli recounted in the *Histoire du Mechique* and culminates in Toad Grandmother's sacrifice and dismemberment at the hands of the hero twins—a close parallel to Tlaltecuhtli's dismemberment by Tezcatlipoca and Quetzalcoatl. As happened in the case of Tlaltecuhtli, all plants and living things sprout from Toad Grandmother's dismembered body (Ibid.:38).

In the relief images of Tlaltecuhtli and in images of other deities in the splayed hocker position, however, there is very little that can be considered toad-like (see Gutiérrez Solana 1983:21, Bonifaz Nuño 1986:64). Even the *chalchihuitl* sign is found on many figures besides toads and does little to confirm a toad reading. In sum, there is very little that directly links Tlaltecuhtli with reptilian, amphibian, or saurian forms. Images of *cipactli* in the hocker position—seen not only in the Aztec world (Figure 13b) but in Olmec and Maya art as well (Figure 13c; see also Covarrubias 1971:f.21)— do illustrate that the surface of the earth was conceived of as the back of a great crocodile. It appears clear, however, that such a figure was considered distinct from Tlaltecuhtli.

Rather than having a single or individual association, it is likely that the hocker position blends several meanings. The splayed body of the earth may symbolize the four world quarters while at the same time uniting themes of birth, defeat, descent, and reptilian or amphibian connections. No single theory precludes the others. Arguments that the position represents death and defeat in battle complement, rather than refute, the arguments that claim it is a position of parturition, for women in childbirth were considered warriors going into battle. Birth and sacrifice thus represent two halves of the same life cycle. Descent, too, carries associations of both life and death, beginnings and endings. Neither does the association with saurian or amphibian creatures, connected so closely to agricultural growth and renewal, somehow contradict or oppose these other theories. Therefore, it may be best to think of the hocker position as having multiple meanings, each of which relates to duality and the mutual dependence of death and life.

Tlaltecuhtli 1

General Features of Tlaltecuhtli 1

The category "Tlaltecuhtli 1" is made up of representations of the female earth. All Tlaltecuhtli 1 images share toothy faces at the elbow and knee joints, a skull and crossbones skirt, *malinalli* grass hair, clawed hands and feet, striated bracelets, and striated anklets edged with bells. The category is further broken down into Tlaltecuhtli 1a (Figures 1-3) and 1b (Figures 4-5), the first marked by a wide-open jaw, the second by an upside-down female head with a knife clenched in her teeth. Overall similarity in the bodies of both types leads to the conclusion that they represent head variants of the same form, although some iconographic variation does occur. These differences, however—including dorsal versus frontal views, skulls clutched in the hands and feet, spotted or unspotted banners, etc.—are considered secondary to the overall similarity among the Tlaltecuhtli 1 variant forms.

One of the most frequently cited characteristics of Tlaltecuhtli 1 is that toothy faces mark the elbow and knee joints. As Seler states, "Its most outstanding and special peculiarity consists of joints of arms and legs that are marked by open, yawning jaws surrounded by teeth without flesh" (1990-[V]:5). This feature is often listed as a diagnostic element of the earth and, when displayed by other gods, is viewed as a sign that these gods are associated with the earth (Heyden 1971:162; Aguilera 2001:40). The *Histoire du Mechique* mentions these masks, "...the goddess Tlaltecuhtli, whose joints were filled with eyes and mouths, with which she bit like a savage beast" (Garibay1973:108). As one of the very few iconographic descriptions of Tlaltecuhtli found in sixteenth-century sources, this passage emphasizes the importance of the masks as a diagnostic feature of Tlaltecuhtli 1. That such masks may have been considered key in the depiction of earth goddesses across Mesoamerican cultures is suggested by a relief from Mayapan, a Postclassic site in the Yucatan, which depicts a frontal female figure with jawed joints (Figure 14a).

In regards to the masked joints of Tlaltecuhtli, Matos Moctezuma (1997:33) and López Austín (1988:166) suggest a connection to Sahagún's descriptions of ash being rubbed onto the joints of a new mother and child to protect them from harm. Arnold explains that a newly delivered mother was considered particularly susceptible to injury through her joints: "Part of a person's vital forces resided in the bones, various spiritual entities penetrated the body through the joints, which were considered weak spots and thus a potential site for the entrance of disease, as well as benign cosmological emanations" (1999:55; see also López Austín 1988:215). These masks may therefore mark Tlaltecuhtli 1 as a newly delivered mother, at risk of pollution by dangerous forces that could attack through her weakened joints. That joints themselves were associated with birth and emergence is seen in page 42 of the Borgia Codex, where figures emerge from the knees and elbows of a skeletal god (Figure 9c).

In contrast, accounts found in Durán (1994) and Acosta (2002) associate these masks with death and funeral rites. Acosta, for instance, describes a funeral ceremony as follows: "Then a priest came out dressed in the accoutrements of the devil, with mouths painted on all the joints and many eyes made of mirrors" (2002:269). What kind of priest this was and what his offices were are not discussed. An account found in Durán is even more vivid: "[Then] came the King and Lord of the Underworld, dressed like a diabolical creature. In place of eyes he wore shining mirrors; his mouth was huge and fierce; his hair was curled; he had two hideous horns; and on each shoulder he wore a mask with mirror eyes. On each elbow there was one of these faces, on his abdomen another, and on his knees still other faces with eyes. With the shining of the mirrors that represented eyes on all these parts, it looked as if he could see in every direction" (1994:308). These masks may, then, have something to do with the omnipresence of Tlaltecuhtli, the fact that her splayed body marked all quarters and the center of the world and, as such, both saw and embodied all directions.

With their goggled eyes and down-curving fanglike teeth, the faces on the joints of Tlaltecuhtli are intriguingly similar to images of *ñuju* figures from the internal pages of the Borgia codex (Figures 14b-d). Though the full meaning of these figures is unknown, they are connected to themes of agricultural growth and fertility. Notable, too, is the fact that, on Borgia Codex pages 30, 33, and 34, these nature spirits are shown with clawed hands and feet, a feature characteristic of earth deities in general and Tlaltecuhtli in particular (Figure 14b). In the Borgia Codex, these *ñuju* faces also mark materials of stone and wood, suggesting that the identical faces on the joints of Tlaltecuhtli may mark her body as a natural substance (Figures 14c-d). The faces of *ñujus* are indistinguishable from that of Tlaloc (Aguilera 2001:40; Bonifaz Nuño 1986:65) and may have been intended to be such, general markers of natural materials that connect their wearers to themes of agriculture and natural abundance. As Alcina Franch argues "...they are merely qualifying adjectives that show the Underworld or terrestrial character of the figures on which they appear" (1995:35).

Though the masks at Tlaltecuhtli's joints are frequently seen in terrestrial contexts, they often appear to be linked to astral or celestial figures as well. As shown in the images from the Codex Tudela page 46r (Figure 15a) and the Codex Magliabechiano page 76r (Figure 15b), such masks were worn by the *tzitzimime* demons. Aguilera (2001:40), for instance, says that Coyolxauhqui (Figure

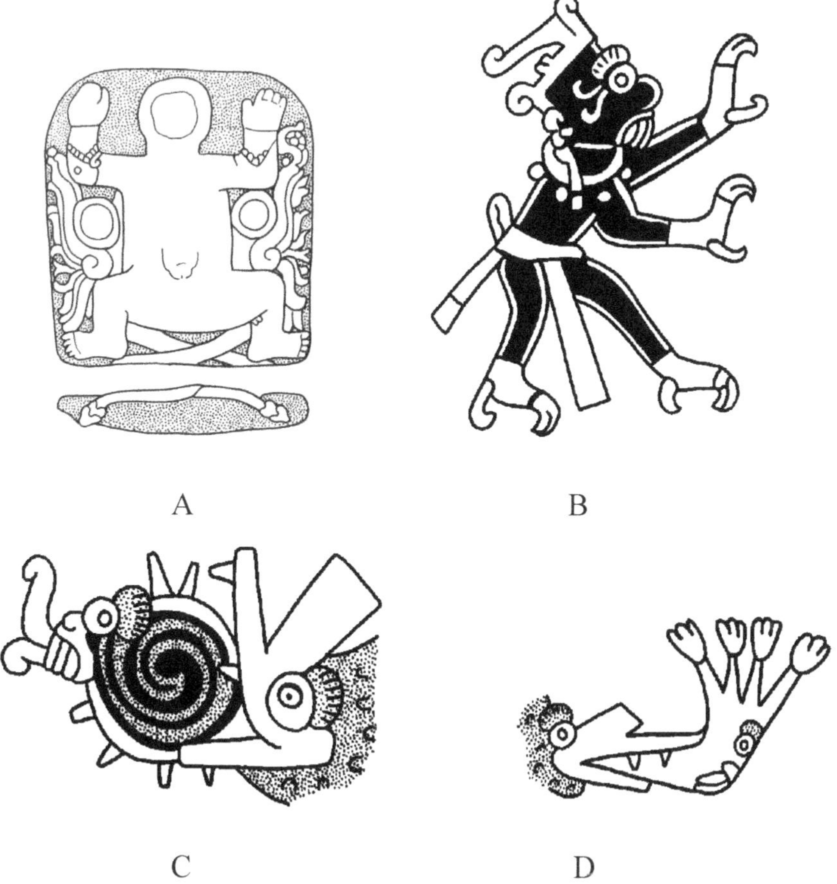

Figure 14: Jawed Joints and *Ñuju* Imagery: a) Earth image from Mayapan (Taube 1993:70); b) *Ñuju* figure piercing day sign (drawing by author after Díaz and Rodgers 1993:pl.30); c) Wind serpent with *ñuju*-faced stone in mouth (drawing by author after Ibid:pl.29);dc) Wind serpent with nuju-faced wood in mouth (drawing by author after Ibid.).

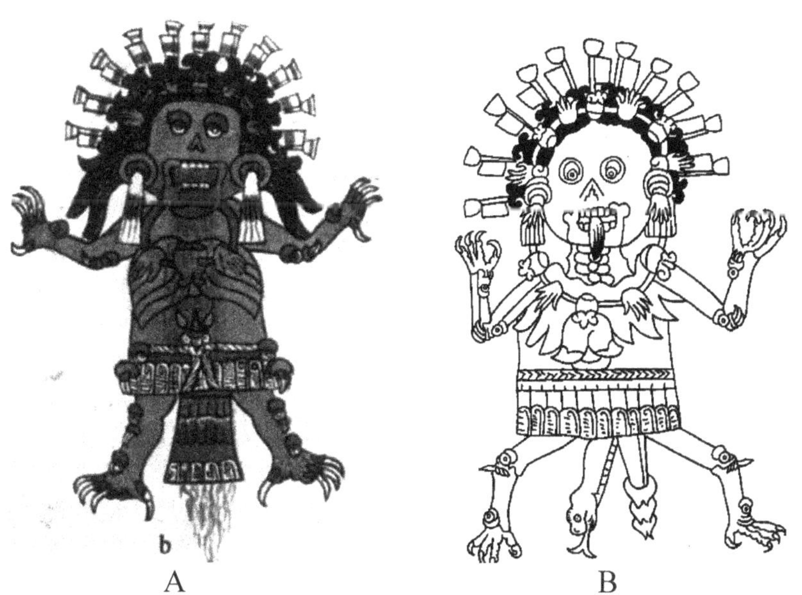

Figure 15: *Tzitzimime* Depictions: a) Tudela 46r (Klein 2000:1b);
b) Magliabechiano 76r (drawing by author after Boone 1983:Folio 97r).

10c) wears these masks on her joints because she is a *cihuateteo* and *tzitzimitl*. Although this seems to contradict an earlier statement that such masks are a diagnostic feature of the earth, Aguilera reconciles the two arguments by recounting the creation myth of Tlaltecuhtli in which one half of the deity's dismembered body becomes the earth and the other the sky. Symbols associated with Tlaltecuhtli may therefore be both terrestrial and celestial signs (Aguilera 2001:40). Another detail that weakens the argument that these masks are straightforward signs of the earth is that images of *cipactli*, the crocodilian earth, do not show such faces (Figures 13b-c). If such masks were a neutral Aztec terrestrial symbol, then images of crocodiles in the hocker position found beneath objects presumably would display them as well.

Perhaps most likely is that these mouths represent the thirsty or hungry nature of the earth. Tlaltecuhtli, after her violent dismemberment by Tezcatlipoca and Quetzalcoatl, cries out to be satiated with the blood and flesh of sacrificial victims. Here one should recall Mendieta's description of Tlaltecuhtli, who the Aztecs depicted "...with mouths on all her joints filled with blood, saying that she ate and swallowed everything" (1945:87). Tlaltecuhtli was not merely a *representation of* the earth in the minds of the Aztecs; Tlaltecuhtli *was* the earth. The ground beneath their feet took on a clear human form. Her entire body, the thirsty earth body that required blood to continue agricultural production, was therefore envisioned as covered with hungry, snapping mouths. *Ñuju*-faced stones and wood found in the pages of the Borgia Codex, though clearly natural materials, are generally associated with castigation and punishment, and, like the earth body of Tlaltecuhtli, would have drunk down their victims' blood. The *tzitzimime* are similarly associated with consumption, namely the devouring of the sun and humankind. These figures, then, like stones and wood, were all imagined as having thirsty, toothy mouths like those covering the body of Tlaltecuhtli.

Another feature shared by Tlaltecuhtli 1 figures is a skirt decorated with a skull and crossbones motif. Such a skeletal design can obviously be linked to death, but it also appears to have been associated with curing and healing, specifically through connections to the *cihuateteo* and *tzitzimime*. Klein, for example, argues "...at least some of the Cihuateteo were associated with a skirt decorated with either a skull or crossed bones" (2000:10). Klein later mentions that such a skirt was also "...diagnostic of the *tzitzimime*" (Ibid.:19). According to Klein (Ibid.), these skirts mark their wearers—predominantly earth goddesses, *cihuateteo*, and *tzitzizmime*—as curers and healers. As a result, these designs were also used to decorate the low-lying platforms where people would call upon these deities to heal them (Ibid.:11) (Figures 16a-b). "It was because these magical garments with their distinctive decorations embodied the powers of these supernaturals that they were materialized in the form of ritual furniture and used to petition for protection from danger and illness" (Ibid.:5). These skirts and platforms are visually equated in three Tlaltecuhtli images (all frontal views of the 1a variant), where skirts are shown as angular, architectural features (Figures 2b-d). These skirts are also bordered by the starry sky bands found on both monolithic stone sculptures and along the borders of skull and crossbones platforms (Figure 16c). These skirts thus connect Tlaltecuhtli 1 images, especially Tlaltecuhtli 1a frontal views, not only to physical architectural features, but also to healing and curing, not to mention the *tzitzimime* and *cihuateteo* as well.

The head of Tlaltecuhtli 1, whether as reptilian maw or decapitated female face, is always crowned by a ruff of tangled hair. This hair, especially in depictions that include the spatulate leaves on their thin stalks, is clearly *malinalli* grass (Peterson 1983:117) and implies that the head of the earth deity, like the earth itself, is covered with a layer of rustling grass. This grass may even have been envisioned as an embodiment of the earth itself. As Peterson states, "The versatile and hardy malinalli grass, able to survive in both arid climates and at higher altitudes, predictable in its perennial return, and fertile in appearance with its heavily seeded flower stalk, early may have come to represent an outward manifestation of the sacred earth..." (Ibid.:123). Due to its practicality and versatility, *malinalli* grass was highly valued by the Aztecs. It was used to make ropes and mats, and was also employed in weaving and tying sacks. The flower stems and leaves of the plant were also used for roofing materials (Ibid.:116), a fact that may have led to the conflation between the roofs of buildings and the hair of the earth. Like Tlaltecuhtli's skull and crossbones skirt, *malinalli* grass associates the deity with healing, for the *malinalli* plant also had medicinal uses (Peterson 1983:126 f.n.17; Klein 2000:14). Quezada (1977:313) notes in particular its use to prevent miscarriage, an application consistent with the general themes of fertility and birth associated with Tlaltecuhtli.

The *malinalli* grass hair shown on Tlaltecuhtli also appears to connect the deity to auto-sacrifice, perhaps even death, as well. The hard stems of the plants, for instance, were used as straws for bloodletting (Peterson 1983:120), while figures of dead lords were crowned during the festival of Tititl, shown on Magliabechiano 60, with *malinalli* grass headdresses (Peterson 1983:118). Nicholson further describes these darker connections of Tlaltecuhtli's *malinalli* grass hair: "This peculiar hair style is a diagnostic of the deities related to death and the underworld and suggests the confused murkiness of night and the darkness of death, when the ever-waiting yawning jaws of 'the father and mother of us all' receive their prey" (1954:166). *Malinalli* grass thus further demonstrates the overall duality embodied by the Aztec earth, uniting the symbolism of life and death, healing and self-sacrifice.

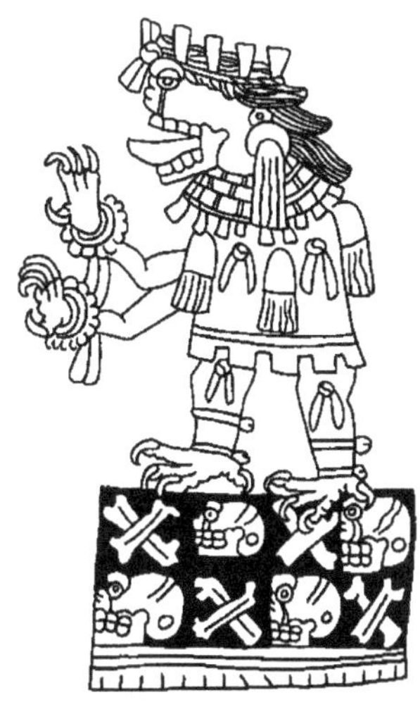

A

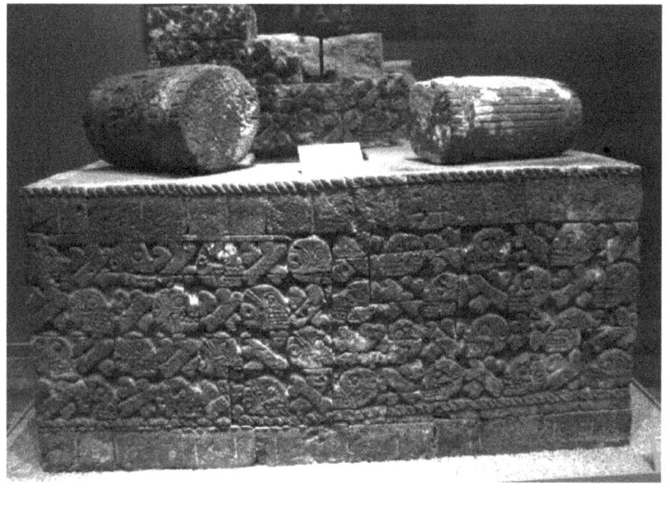

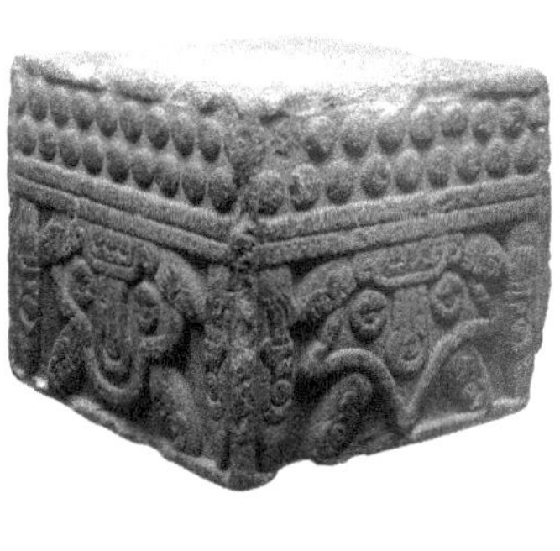

B

C

Figure 16: Skirts as Platforms: a) Codex Magliabechiano (drawing by author after Boone 1983:76); b) Aztec skull and crosed-bones platform (photo by author); c) Aztec cube marked with Venus signs identical to those of the skirts of Figures 2b and 2c (Matos Moctezuma and Solís 2002:f.136).

Dorsal Tlaltecuhtli 1a and 1b images also occasionally display insects, including spiders, centipedes, and worms, in their *malinalli* hair (Figures 1a-b, 4c-d). In an obvious sense, these creatures, which live in soil and dark places, represent those things that inhabit the earth. As Taube (pers. comm. 2004) notes, in order to see images of Tlaltecuhtli—so often carved beneath objects—one would have had to lift the object off the ground, leaving moist dirt and wriggling insects behind. The centipede, for its part, is considered a liminal creature, associated with the darkness of the underworld and earth entrances, while the spider is associated with both earth and sky, terrestrial and lunar deities. On the one hand, the spider is connected with weaving and creative, productive enterprises, and on the other with the *tzitzimime* demons, who were believed to descend to earth during solar eclipses to wreak havoc upon mankind. Both the centipede and scorpion were similarly associated with the *tzitzimime* as well as the *cihuateteo* (Klein 1976:131-134).

These creatures also carry associations of black magic and death. Durán, for instance, describes Malinalxochitl as using them to kill her enemies, "With magic spells, she slays those who anger her by sending snakes and scorpions, centipedes, or deadly spiders to bite them" (1994:24). Moctezuma used a similar technique in efforts to assassinate Cortes (Ibid:513), though they unfortunately proved ineffective. Klein discusses the presence of these various insects in the hair of female goddesses as tools of witchcraft and sorcery, used to bewitch and seduce unsuspecting men (Klein 2000:14 n.35, 1994:225,229). These creatures, however, were also associated with rites of healing. Durán, for example, talks of the ritual soot that Aztec priests and rulers smeared on their faces, which was derived from ash, "...scorpions, spiders, centipedes, other unpleasant little creatures, tobacco, and the seed of *ololiuhqui*... This mixture was supposed to protect the persons upon whom it was smeared from all dangers" (1994:189 f.n.2). These creatures, then, represent the delicate balance between death and protection. As Klein states, the earth's "...*malinalli* hair and its contents, therefore, would have connoted not just the dangers threatening pregnant women but also the goddess's potential to assist them" (2000:14).[12]

Other features characteristic of Tlaltecuhtli 1 are her clawed hands and feet and the striated bracelets and anklets that she wears. Both features unfortunately have meanings that are difficult to understand at present. On the one hand, the claws of Tlaltecuhtli might be jaguar claws, which would associate Tlaltecuhtli 1 with terrestrial themes, as well as darkness and night. On the other hand, a number of authors argue that they are eagle claws, citing either that there is one rear talon (Boone 1999:190) or that there are four total talons (Townsend 1979:67) as evidence of the fact. Seler's statement that the *tzitzimime* descend to earth in the form of eagles (1963 [II]:20) may also support an avian identity for these claws. As opposed to the terrestrial jaguar, the eagle is a solar body and embodies astral or celestial themes.

Around her wrists and ankles Tlaltecuhtli wears what Nicholson identifies in one article as "striated skin cuffs" (1967:82) and, in another, as leather bracelets worn most often by deities associated with the west (1954:166). The anklets are often edged with small bells. If these wristlets and anklets are indeed made of skin, they may link Tlaltecuhtli 1a to the ritual flaying of sacrificial victims in rites of agricultural renewal, connected to the god Xipe Totec as well as the mother goddess Toci. In these rites, the donning of the flayed skin by the presiding priest was considered analogous to the dressing of the fields with the green of new agricultural growth. While the agricultural connections of such an adornment as skin bracelets are consistent with the previously discussed associations of Tlaltecuhtli, more iconographic evidence is needed to support such a definite identification. Aguilera, for instance, points out that the bracelets worn by Coyolxauhqui (Figure 10c)—bracelets identical to those seen on the wrists of Tlaltecuhtli 1a—were important accessories of battle, protecting warriors against sprains by reinforcing the wrists and, on the left side, helping to secure a shield (2001:33). This alternate reading would emphasize themes of warfare over those of agriculture. The iconographic similarity between some of the anklets worn by Tlaltecuhtli 1 and depictions of coyote fur anklets from images of warriors may further support this connection to war.

Tlaltecuhtli 1a: Consumption, Caves, and Sacrifice

The Tlaltecuhtli 1a subgroup, shown in both frontal and dorsal views, is most easily recognized by her wide-open reptilian maw, filled with sharp teeth and curving fangs. I believe this variant represents the truest form of Tlaltecuhtli, the most straightforward depiction of the Aztec earth. Both the Mixtec codices and the Borgia group, for instance, are replete with images of this wide-open maw as symbol of the earth, indicating that this head variant should be understood as a widespread Mexican conception of the earth (see Gutiérrez Solana 1983:24). Some authors connect this head to images of *cipactli*, the earth crocodile, arguing that Tlaltecuhtli 1a is composed of two profile *cipactli* heads. As Klein states, "Tlaltecuhtli thus typically shares with Cipactli a missing lower jaw, sharp pointed teeth, a curled nose and curled eyebrow, and a flint knife projecting from the nose" (Klein 1977:187). Klein also links it to the head of the colossal "Coatlicue," arguing for the possibility that the head of Tlaltecuhtli 1a is composed of two bloodstreams (1988:243).

Throughout the Borgia group and Mixtec codices, the jaws of the earth are shown gulping down mummy bundles (Figure 17a-b; see also Codex Laud page 21v). In many examples, too, sacrificed victims are portrayed tumbling head first into the earth's gaping jaws (Figure 17c; see also Codex Laud page 15v). In relief sculpture, then, the open maw of Tlaltecuhtli 1a designates her as the all-consuming earth, devourer of the dead. The Aztecs viewed the earth as both the beginning and the end of the cycle of life, womb and tomb (Nicholson 1971:422), dual associations that are found throughout Mesoamerica. The Tzotzil, for instance, believe that the earth "...brings forth and fosters all creatures, but is simultaneously their common grave. She relentlessly swallows back, as a monster, the beings that she produces... She is all-producing, all maintaining, all-devouring" (Guiteras-Holmes 1961:189). The open jaws of Tlaltecuhtli 1a thereby relate this variant to metaphors of death and consumption. As Nicholson states, "This grotesque creature, Tlaltecuhtli, was possibly believed to swallow the sun in the evening, disgorging it each dawn, also devouring the blood and hearts of sacrificed victims and the souls of the dead in general" (1971:406).

Throughout Mesoamerica, death is associated with metaphors of consumption. For the Tzotzil of Chenalho, for example, death is attributed to the *nagual*, or animal soul, being eaten (Guiteras Holmes 1961:139-40), while in Yucatec Mayan the word for sacrifice translates as "to open the mouth," possibly a reference to the ritual

[12] It is interesting to note that such creatures are missing from frontal Tlaltecuhtli 1a images, whose architectural skirts connect them so closely to medicine, curing, and the platforms used for healing rituals.

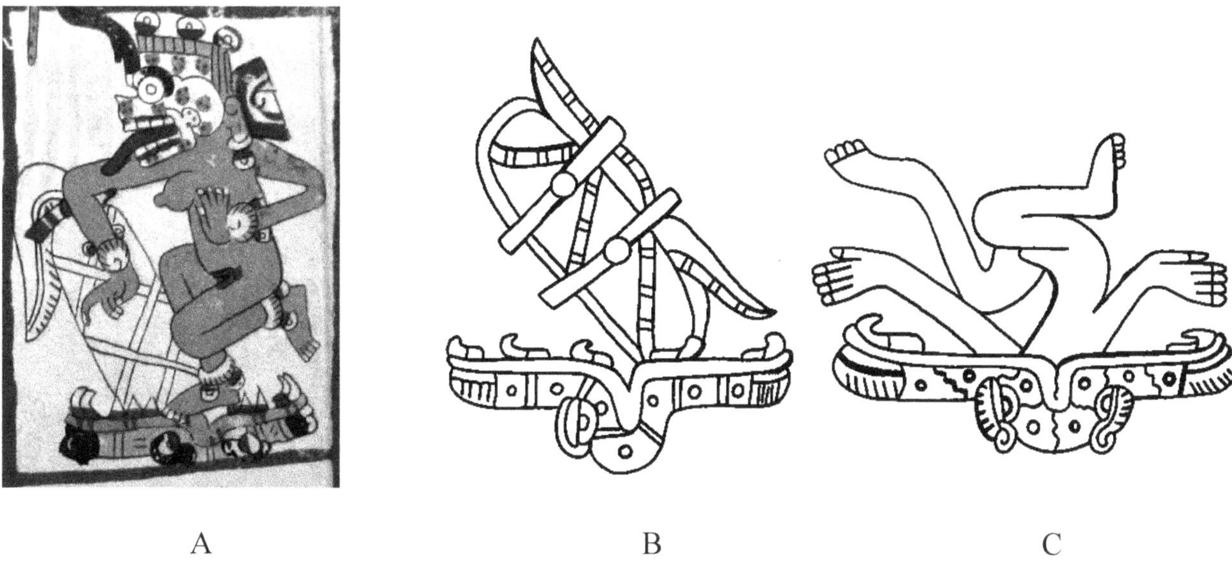

Figure 17: Codex Depictions of the Jaws of the Earth: a) Codex Vaticanus B page 90; b) Codex Borgia page 13 (drawing by author after Díaz and Rodgers 1993:pl.13); c) CodexBorgia page 60 (drawing by author after Díaz and Rodgers 1993:pl.60).

smearing of blood onto the mouths of deity figures (Thompson 1970:175). The belief that one was consumed by the earth at death is further demonstrated in Durán's description of the emperor Axayacatl's funeral in which a guest states, "There you lie, there you rest in the... nine mouths of death..." (1994:292). The reciprocal relationship of consumption between the earth and mankind may be reinforced through the ceremonial eating of earth, *tlalqualiztli*, often seen in contexts of prisoner sacrifice, when those to be sacrificed thrust their finger into the earth and ate the dirt that stuck to it (Durán 1994:327, 288). This action alludes to the mutual responsibilities of humans, who eat the products of the earth, and the earth, who eats the bodies of the dead. "We eat of the earth/ then the earth eats us" (Knab 1983, quoted in Broda 1987:107).

The earth, often paired with the sun, was considered an important consumer of sacrificial offerings. As Sahagún records in a prayer to Tezcatlipoca: "The earth god opens his mouth, thirsty to drink the blood of the many who will die in this war. It seems that the sun and the earth god called Tlaltecuhtli want to celebrate. They will give food and drink to the gods of heaven and of hell, inviting them to partake of the flesh and blood of the men who will die in this war" (cited by Matos Moctezuma 1995:29). In the *Histoire du Mechique*, this view of the earth as demanding human sacrifice is also made clear: "It was added that this goddess at times cried out at night and demanded hearts of humans, and that she would not bring forth fruit until she was soaked in blood" (Seler 1990-[V]:5; see also Garibay 1973). That so many of the currently known examples of Tlaltecuhtli relief carvings are found on the bottoms of *cuauhxicalli* sacrificial vessels, known to have been receptacles for human hearts, also speaks for the role of this deity as the great consumer of human blood offerings.

Along with metaphors of consumption, the toothy maw of Tlaltecuhtli may also allude to the jagged entrances of caves. Throughout Mesoamerica, caves were seen as entrances into the earth. Consequently, they are often shown as open, toothy mouths (Figure 18a). Caves were also used as receptacles for the dead. Sahagún, for instance, states that the skins of flayed victims were often placed in caves (1950-82[II]:5), while Heyden argues, "The pictorial codices showing mummy bundles placed in the mouth of the earth often represent cave burials" (1976:22). Caves, then, quite literally consumed the deceased. The north wall of the newly discovered Preclassic mural at San Bartolo in the Maya area exquisitely portrays the Mesoamerican conflation of caves and open monster jaws (Figure 18b). Here, the under-painting reveals that the muralist at first outlined an inward-curving monster fang in the upper jaw, but later replaced it with an extraordinarily realistic depiction of a stalactite (Saturno, et al. 2005).

Caves are also seen as great earth wombs. Girard, for instance, describes "...the cave, which symbolizes the center or navel of the world, which is, at the same time, the vagina of the earth goddess" (1966:75). This blending of caves and wombs is best illustrated in the famous depiction of the migration from Chicomoztoc from the *Historia Tolteca Chichimeca*, which portrays the seven-lobed cave of origin as a fleshy, multi-chambered womb (Figure 18c). That mouths and wombs were sometimes visually conflated is demonstrated in page 41 of the Vaticanus B, which shows a death goddess with an umbilical cord emerging from her mouth (Figure 18d).

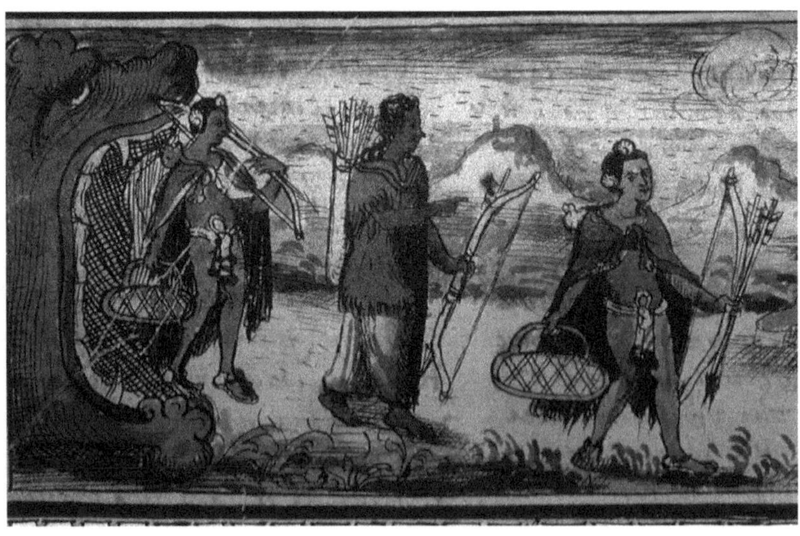

A

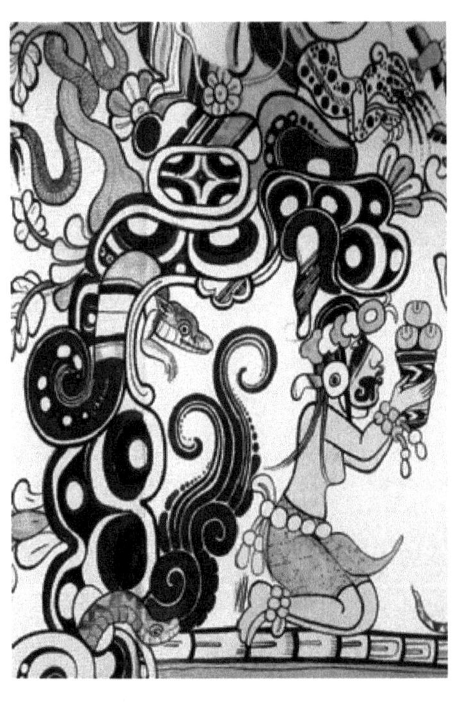

B

C

Figure 18: Cave Imagery, Mouths and Wombs: a) Emergence from the monster mouth of Chicomoztoc (Durán 1994:pl.3); b) San Bartolo emergence scene (note stalactite fang) (Rendering by Heather Hearst, courtesy of the Boundary End Archaeology Research Center, Barnardsville, North Carolina); c) Emergence from the womb of Chicomoztoc (Solís 2004:95);

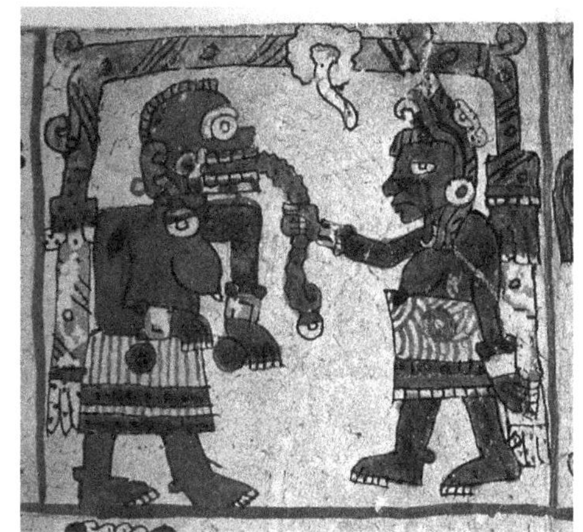
D

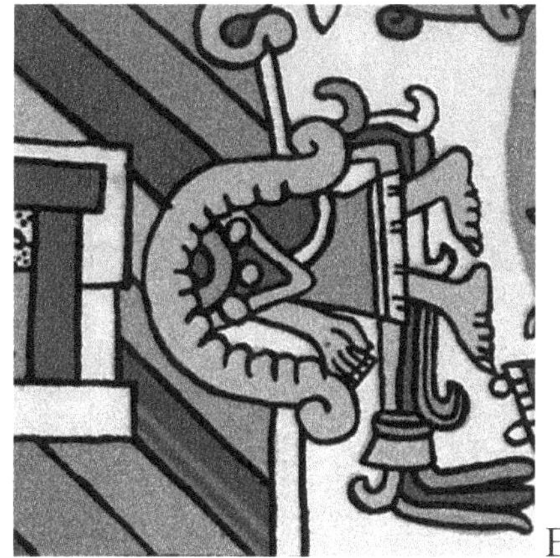
E

Figure 18 continued: d) Death goddess with umbilicus from mouth (Codex Vaticanus B page 41); e) Figure entering cave womb (Nuttall 1975:16).

The Huichol creation myth which deals with the great contests of creation between Sun Father and Grandmother Growth shows that toothy wombs are also known ethnographically. In this tale, Grandmother Earth creates the first females, but Sun Father places teeth in their vaginas to prevent them from procreating. Therefore, it is conceivable that the Aztecs, too, conceived of the opening of the earth as not only a toothy maw but a toothy vagina as well (see Matos Moctezuma 1997).

Generally speaking, however, mouths are more associated with death and consumption than birth and emergence. In art, then, figures most often fall into mouths in death and emerge from wombs in birth. There are three important exceptions to this broad rule. The first is an image from the Nuttall Codex in which a woman enters the earth womb headfirst (Figure 18e). The second is the previously mentioned scene at San Bartolo, in which the first people bring foodstuffs out of the cave mouth (Figure 18b). Third is the well-known scene from Durán's *Historia de las Indias de Nueva España* in which the first humans are shown emerging from the great monster mouth of Chicomoztoc (Figure 18a). Generally speaking, however, a great, open mouth can usually be equated with the jaws of death, or entry into the earth, while vaginas or wombs are associated with birth. Consequently, while the open mouth of Tlaltecuhtli may associate her both with death and birth, it should be emphasized that the former is by far the principal association, marking Tlaltecuhtli 1a first and foremost as a consumer of the dead.

Tlaltecuhtli 1a is most often shown with her back to the viewer, a perspective indicated by the skull ornament that she wears. In this view, the skull and crossbones skirt is deemphasized, wrapped tightly underneath the buttocks and around the thighs of the goddess, the hem shown at an angle over each leg. The skull back ornament, which along with the skull and crossbones skirt identifies Tlaltecuhtli 1a as female, distinguishes this dorsal view from frontal Tlaltecuhtli 1a depictions. As shown in codex depictions as well as in several three-dimensional stone sculptures, this skull is invariably worn on the back of female deities (Figure 10) and therefore, in Tlaltecuhtli imagery, must indicate that the viewer is seeing Tlaltecuhtli from behind. In most depictions, this skull is ornamented by a flap of jaguar skin, from which hang braided rope or cloth tassels, often finished by a row of seashells.

The skull itself is usually shown in profile, although several images do show it frontally, and emphasizes Tlaltecuhtli's association with decapitation and sacrifice. The skull, both when frontal and in profile, is shown pierced through the temple by a belt (Figures 19a-b). Marked in a number of cases as the skin or undulating body of a serpent, this belt is iconographically identical to the serpent belts frequently worn by female deities throughout Central Mexico.[13] In the case of Tlaltecuhtli, this belt also likely represents a rail of the *tzompantli* skull rack, upon which the skulls of decapitated sacrificial victims were threaded (Figure 19c). Festivals to the earth goddesses inevitably included the death of the deity impersonator by decapitation (Klein 1988:243; Joyce 2000:166), and it is therefore not inconceivable that these skull ornaments signify the sacrifice of earth deities or deity impersonators to ensure agricultural fertility. *Tzompantli* racks themselves represented themes of agricultural abundance and were seen as "artificial orchards" (Baquedano and Graulich 1993:164 f.n.2) because "the wooden racks with their rotting heads were supposed to be fruit trees with ripe fruit" (Ibid.).

[13] Boone, in a discussion of the colossal "Coatlicue" describes this wavy pattern, found on the necklace of the figure, as indicating blood (1999:191). Baquedano and Graulich link the two themes, discussing serpents as connected to, among other things, menstrual blood when shown between the legs (1993:169). Therefore, such a pattern could mark Tlaltecuhtli's belt as both serpentine and sanguinary.

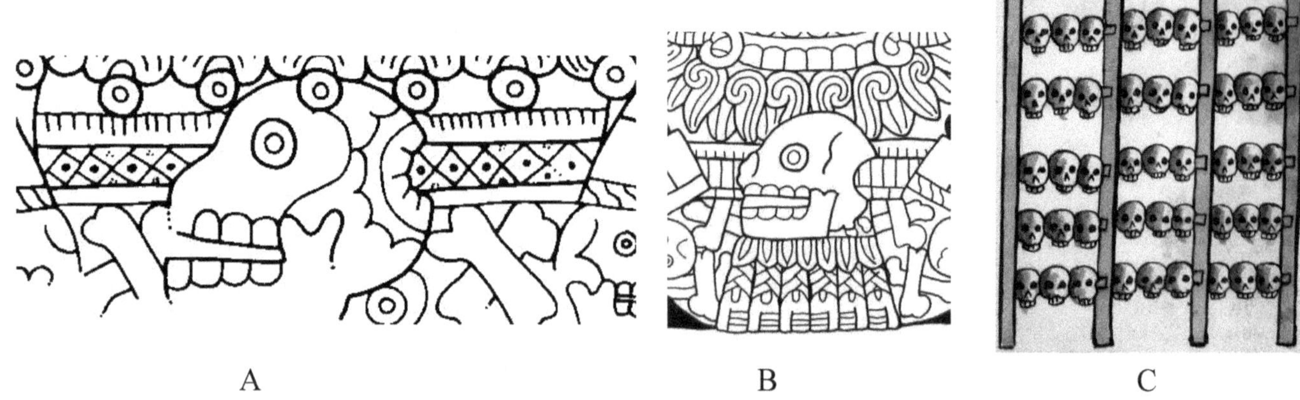

Figure 19: *Tzompantli* and Decapitation Imagery: a-b) Back skulls worn by Tlaltecuhtli 1a (drawing by author after Nicholson and Quiñones Keber 1983:42; Taube 1993:36); c) *Tzompantli* skull rack from Tovar Codex (Solís 2004:143).

This dorsal view of Tlaltecuhtli also depicts paper banners hanging from the deity's wrists, features that connect her to victims of sacrifice. Such associations are discussed in a following section.

The Tlaltecuhtli 1a "Knife Variant":

An interesting subset of Tlaltecuhtli 1a dorsal views—referred to as the "knife variant" (Figure 3)—is identified by several features, first among them a blade, at times personified, which emerges from the deity's mouth.[14] In this subset, the teeth are all curved and sometimes rise out from a gum, as opposed to the more generic form of Tlaltecuhtli 1a that exhibits straight teeth rising directly from the lips. Another distinguishing feature is that this figure, along with the masked joints so characteristic of Tlaltecuhtli 1 images, wears skulls, pierced through the temple and lashed onto her forearms and lower legs. These skulls have a double outline characteristic of Gulf Coast scrollwork and connect this image to Tlaltecuhtli 2. Like Tlaltecuhtli 1a dorsal views, the "knife variant" also shows paper banners, symbols of sacrifice, attached to the wrists.

It may be of some interest to note here that several Tlaltecuhtli 1a images show the deity's teeth as obsidian blades, and several "knife variant" images similarly depict the central blade as obsidian. In Aztec art, flint and obsidian are easily distinguished, for flint is marked by a clear serrated edge, while obsidian blades are shown as having smooth surfaces, the ends sometimes demarcated with a line to show that they were tipped with blood (K. Taube, personal communication 2004). Several pieces of evidence suggest that such a distinction is meaningful. Obsidian, for instance, was connected with decapitation and dismemberment, including the dismemberment and removal of a dead fetus to save a mother's life (Aguilera 2001:29, 37; Madsen 1960:10; Quezada 1977:314; Sahagún 1950-82[VI]:160). Heyden discusses the black color of obsidian as a color that makes one invisible, invincible, and protected, and mentions that it was also associated with vegetation, rain, mother earth, and creation (1974:12; 1976:25). Graulich notes, "Cold, black obsidian is exactly the opposite of warm, white flint" (1997:108). Therefore, while obsidian was used for decapitation and dismemberment, flint was used for heart sacrifice (Motolinía 1970:32; Sahagún 1950-82[II]:47). "In opposition to flint, black, cold and nocturnal obsidian was considered as coming from the inside of the earth and, therefore, perfectly fitted for the rituals on behalf of Tlaltecuhtli" (Graulich 1988:402). Heart excision, on the other hand "...was a sacrifice to heavenly fire and to carry it out only a flint knife could be used, for flint was or contained a spark descended from heaven" (Ibid.:401).

The blade that emerges from the mouth of the Tlaltecuhtli 1a "knife variant" may represent a symbolic tongue. Klein, for instance, discusses knife tongues as "biting" into flesh and also notes the ties between knives and mouths in Mayan languages (Klein 1976:204 f.n.1). That these knife tongues may have been associated with death and sacrifice, particularly decapitation, is shown in Aztec offertory caches, where eyes and a flint nose and tongue were often added to skulls (Figure 20a). Therefore, the knife tongue would associate this Tlaltecuhtli 1a variant with death and decapitation, likening her head to that of a decapitated sacrificial victim.

If mouths, especially the mouth of the earth goddess, were conceptually linked to wombs—jagged cave wombs in particular—then these central knives may also be shown being born out of the womb of the earth. Strange as this might sound, such events are discussed throughout Aztec myth, where female goddesses are often associated with the birth of blades. For example, Cihuacoatl and Citlalinicue are discussed as giving birth to knives rather than babies. Caso, for instance, notes that the Aztec people knew when Cihuacoatl had passed because she

[14] Gutiérrez Solana (1983) appears to be the first author to have made a distinction between this variant and other Tlaltecuhtli 1 forms.

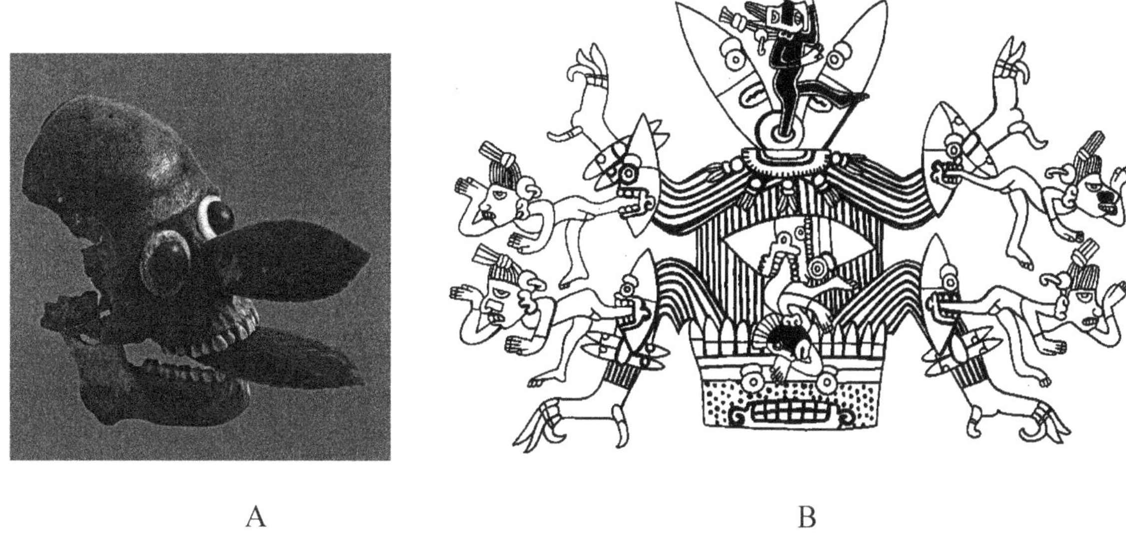

A B

Figure 20: Flint Imagery: a) Flint nose and tongue added to skull (Solís 2004:f.73); b) Birth from flint-headed god (note hips as bowl) (drawing by author after Díaz and Rodgers 1993:pl.32).

would leave an empty cradle with a sacrificial knife next to it (1970:54, see also Brundage 1979:169, 1972:97,98, 99-100, 161). Nuttall discusses the office of the Cihuacoatl in similar terms, describing its emblem as "...the flint knife, the offspring of Cihuacoatl, the earth-mother" (1901:62). Itzpapalotl is sometimes discussed as dying in the process of giving birth to a knife or bursting into a shower of multicolored flints at her death (Klein 1993, 1994:231, 2000:16; Broda 1987:86; Brundage 1979:171). Especially in the case of Itzpapalotl, these births should be seen as events of self-sacrifice which take place in order to provide a means of nourishing the sun and earth with human blood, namely flint and obsidian knives.

The myth of Citlalicue links knives themselves to creation, for the knife birthed by the goddess is expelled from heaven by its embarrassed siblings; it falls to earth, specifically Chicomoztoc, and shatters, becoming the 1600 heroes (Mendieta 1945:83, Graulich 1997:106). Broda discusses the importance of flint knives as symbols of origins and beginnings (1987:85), a theory consistent with images from Borgia page 32 (Figure 20b) and Vindobonensis page 49d, which show deities and other figures born out of flint knives. This sort of imagery is linked especially closely with Xipe Totec, who is associated with the earth through shared connections to agricultural growth and renewal and is often depicted as a personified blade. The flint blade, as a means of flaying, represented a means of restoring the new green skin to the earth.

Though knives are clearly connected to growth and renewal, however, I believe that they should be understood, first and foremost, as instruments of sacrifice—by heart extraction, decapitation, and flaying. That they are associated with new beginnings and agricultural renewal is because they act initially and primarily as symbols of sacrifice. Therefore, in Tlaltecuhtli 1a images, the deity's jaws are filled with the primary instruments of sacrifice—flint and obsidian blades—that were used to nourish the sun and earth with blood.

Importantly, all of the Tlaltecuhtli images found beneath *cuauhxicalli* exhibit the "knife variant," so the emergence of the blade, whether as tongue or as a newborn, connect this variant to blood sacrifice and the offering of blood to the gods. The flint could be both tongue and newborn in this case; the former would mark her as sacrificial victim (recalling the origins of Tlaltecuhtli and the deity's dismemberment by Quetzalcoatl and Tezcatlipoca) while the latter identifies her as the great mother of sacrifice. She is both the means of giving blood to the gods as well as their first victim.

Frontal Views of Tlaltecuhtli 1a

There are four frontal views of Tlaltecuhtli 1, all of which are found on relief panels and all of which fall under the Tlaltecuhtli 1a heading (Figure 2) (though the base of the Stuttgart statuette (Figure 5d) is a possible exception). In these frontal Tlaltecuhtli 1a images, the skull back ornament is obviously missing. The skull and crossbones skirt, on the other hand, is emphasized, its architectural form connecting it to the previously discussed platforms used for rites of healing and curing. Because it is bordered by star imagery, Seler suggests that this skirt may be the *citlalcueitl*, or "starry skirt" discussed in the *Florentine Codex* as a costuming feature of female deities (1963[II]:180; see also Nicholson 1954:166-167). However, as Sahagún never explicitly describes this skirt in visual terms, it is difficult to know for certain.

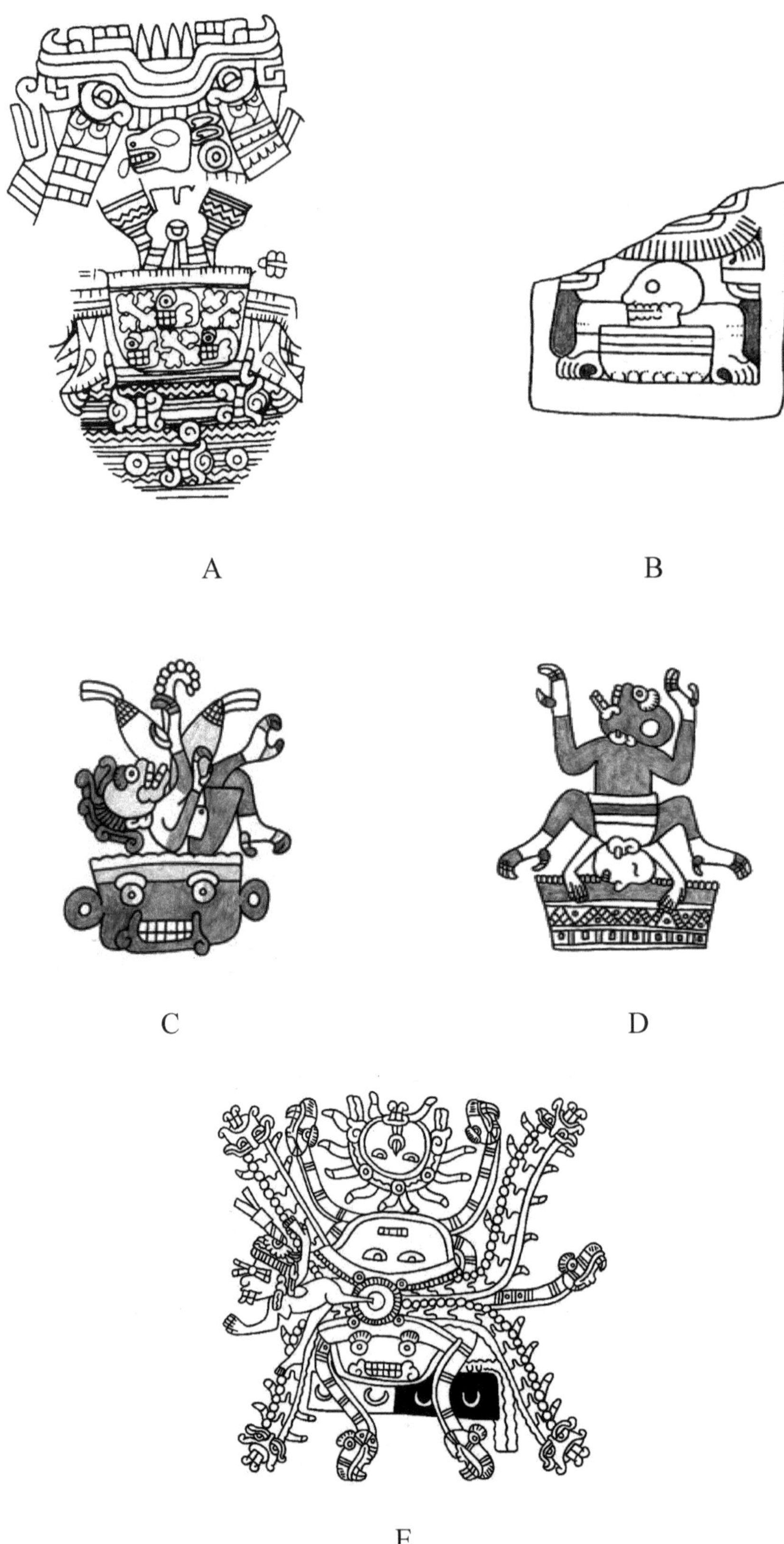

Figure 21: Skirts and Hips as Bowls, Bowls as Wombs: a) Base of Bilimek Vessel (drawing by author after Pasztory 1983:pl.282); b) Possible Tlaltecuhtli variant with bowl instead of hips (drawing by author after Seler 1990-[IV]:232, f.47); c) skeletal goddess born from a bowl (Borgia page 31, drawing by author from Díaz and Rodgers 1993); d) birth scene showing hips as a bowl, taking place on top of a bowl (Borgia page 40, drawing by author after Ibid.); e) Birth scene from body of *cihuateotl* showing womb as bowl (drawing by author after Ibid.:pl. 47).

While in three cases the skirt of frontal Tlaltecuhtli 1a is presented as an architectural feature, in one case it is instead shaped like a bowl (Figure 21a). Another example shows a Tlaltecuhtli variant figure with a similar bowl-skirt form (Figure 21b). Taube discusses the fact that, throughout Mesoamerica, sacrificial bowls were considered symbolic wombs: "...it is likely that *cuauhxicalli* symbolized the womb and birth canal of the earth, the place from which the sun was daily born" (2004:173). The Huichol, for instance, envision their offering bowls as wombs of the earth mother. The sun symbol on the interior of these bowls replicates the birth of the sun through the womb of the earth, just as Maya bowls associated with scenes of birth are so often marked with the *k'in* sign. This positioning of sun symbols inside of *cuauhxicalli* bowls indicates that the Tlaltecuhtli 1a "knife variant" was conceived of in three dimensions. Always depicted in a dorsal view, she was conceived of as lying on her back beneath the bowl, with the sun emerging in birth on the interior of the bowl, her symbolic womb.

The Aztecs had similar associations of bowls with wombs, a connection illustrated in the myth of Quetzalcoatl's return with the bones of the previous creation: "And when he had brought [the bones], the one named Quilaztli, Cihuacoatl, ground them up. Then she put them into a jade bowl and Quetzalcoatl bled his penis on them" (Bierhorst 1992:146; see also Matos Moctezuma 1995:42). In this myth the blood of Quetzalcoatl is analogous to semen, while the bowl serves as the symbolic womb of the earth goddess Cihuacoatl. In the Borgia codex, skirts or hips are often conceived of as vessels, a conflation emphasized by the birth of deities and other figures from bowls (Figures 21c-e).

Again, however, imagery of birth is often paralleled by that of death. The dead, for instance, especially infants, were often buried in vessels in Mesoamerica. Just as vessels, like *cuauhxicalli*, were often filled with water or blood, the earth womb was considered a watery place, symbolic both of the amniotic fluid during pregnancy as well as the watery Underworld inhabited by the dead. That is why, as Matos Moctezuma discusses, burial and the travels of the soul through the Underworld reenact, in reverse, pregnancy and birth: "Thus it was not unusual for a corpse to be placed with its legs bent, to be buried in what specialists call the fetal position, and for the body to be sprinkled with water. It was a form of returning to the same position and ambience it had before birth" (1995:33; 1997).

The primary feature that marks these images of Tlaltecuhtli 1a as frontal views is the presence of the *chalchihuitl* sign on her abdomen, though in one case, the *chalchihuitl* is replaced by an *ollin* sign. That these signs are placed on the abdomens of three-dimensional sculptures of toads (Figure 13a) demonstrates that they do, indeed, indicate frontal views (Nicholson and Quiñones Keber 1983:116). The *chalcihuitl*, symbol of preciousness and fertility, marks the center of the earth's body as the "turquoise enclosure," the "navel of the earth" (Sahagún 1950-82[I]:84, [VI]:19) from which all living things emerge (see López Austin 1988:173). One relief of Tlaltecuhtli 1a, for instance, shows the god Tezcatlipoca, naked like a newborn, stepping out from the *chalchihuitl*-marked earth womb (Figure 2b). This position also indicates birth in the Codex Borgia, where figures are frequently shown in similar scenes of emergence from *chalchihuitl* signs (Figure 9b). Nicholson (1954:170; 1967) links this imagery to the creation myth recounted in the *Histoire du Mechique* in which Tezcatlipoca and Quetzalcoatl enter the body of Tlaltecuhtli through the mouth and navel, respectively, to raise the sky from the deity's collapsed body.

The Features and Face of Tlaltecuhtli 1b

Tlaltecuhtli 1b is almost always shown in a dorsal pose and the body of the deity is, in many ways, indistinguishable from dorsal Tlaltecuhtli 1a depictions, showing the same jawed joints, clawed hands and feet, skull and crossbones skirt, "skin cuffs," paper banners, and *malinalli* hair (Figures 4-5). Her main point of divergence is that she bears a female face, oriented upside-down in a position of decapitation. This face is marked by circles on the cheeks, a skeletal jaw, a personified blade clenched in the teeth, round earflares, and a striated headband that separates the forehead from the *malinalli* hair. Although the meaning of this headband is rather elusive, it gives the impression that the *malinalli* hair worn by Tlaltecuhtli 1b is strapped on like a headdress, perhaps alluding to the wearing of *malinalli* headdresses by dead lords at the Tititl festival (Peterson 1983:118).

Klein identifies the face of Tlaltecuhtli 1b as that of Cihuacoatl-Ilamatecuhtli (1980; 2000:12, Fig. 10b). It is difficult to find support for such a specific identification, however, because Tlaltecuhtli 1b lacks the main attributes that so often set Cihuacoatl-Ilamatecuhtli apart from more generic earth goddesses, specifically the weaving batten, shield, and feathered headdress topped by two flint blades seen in the Borbonicus and Magliabechiano codices (Figure 22). That such features were considered key to the identity of Cihuacoatl is illustrated by Sahagún, who mentions the eagle feather headdress and weaving stick as attributes of Cihuacoatl (1950-82[I]:11). As these represent the main attributes that distinguish Cihuacoatl from other female deities, it is difficult to argue for a Cihuacoatl identity without them. A small detail that is also worthy of mention is Aguilera's brief statement that decapitation was not associated with the astral Cihuacoatl and was related to terrestrial and solar deities instead (1978). That Tlaltecuhtli 1b is shown as a decapitated victim, then, also brings the Cihuacoatl identification into question.

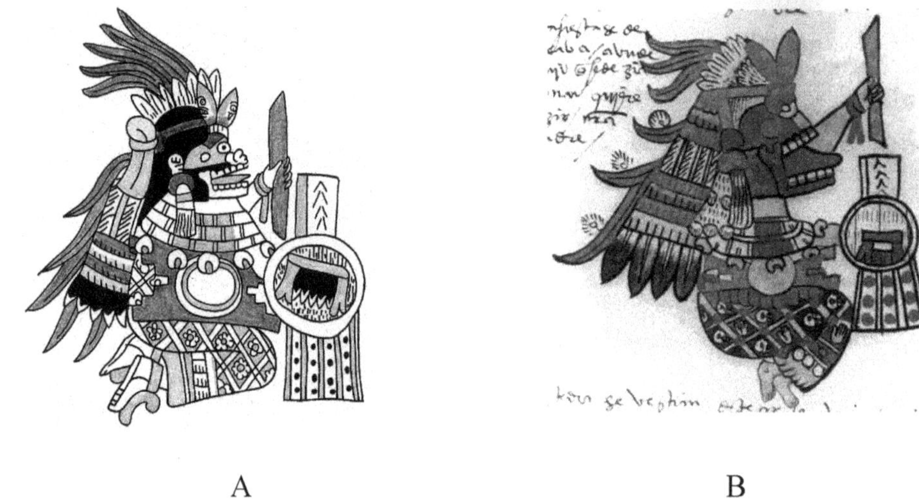

A B

Figure 22: Images of Cihuacoatl: a) Magliabechiano 33 (drawing by author after Boone 1983:33); b) Codex Tudela 27r (Klein 2000:f.11).

Because Tlaltecuhtli 1b exhibits all of the more generic traits of the *cihuateteo* and *tzitzimime*, including a skeletal jaw, tangled malinalli hair, and a flint blade clenched in her teeth (see Heyden 1974:3), I believe that this is more likely the face of a *cihuateotl* or *tzitzimitl*. The *tzitzimime* were female demons associated with childbirth and healing (Klein 2000) as well as chaos and destruction. "There was great fear. It was said that if [the moon] finished eating the sun, so it was said, all would be in darkness; the *tzitzimime* would descend here; they would devour us" (Sahagún 1997:153). It was also believed that these astral demons would descend at the end of the Fifth Sun, when earthquakes destroyed the world, to devour mankind. The *cihuateteo*, women warriors killed in the battle of birth, brought the sun from its zenith to setting, and, consequently, were held responsible for his death every night. As Sahagún states, "...the women then began; they carried, they brought down the sun... They left it there, it is said, where the sun enters. It was said they delivered it into the hands of... the people of Mictlan... that is, the dead..."(1950-82[VI]:163).

The Tlaltecuhtli image carved into the base of the Stuttgart statuette (Figure 5d) may exhibit even closer *tzitzimime* connections. This image, which represents a possible exception to the rule that Tlaltecuhtli 1b is always shown in a dorsal view, is further distinguishable from other Tlaltecuhtli 1b images due to the fact that her entire face is skeletal, rather than just her jaw. The alabaster rendition of Tlaltecuhtli 1b (Figure 5b), though heavily eroded and only published in a low quality photograph, appears to have the same round skeletal eyes and defleshed nose as the Stuttgart image. These two depictions of Tlaltecuhtli 1b may therefore be more directly connected to either the *tzitzimime* demons or the *cihuateteo*. Their iconographic similarity to the *tzitzimime* portrayed in the codices, for instance, is easy to see (Figure 15). These Tlaltecuhtli 1b figures, however, do lack the paper banners seen in the hair of *tzitzimime* depictions, and *tzitzimime* are generally shown without the skull back ornament so typical of Tlaltecuhtli.

Tlaltecuhtli 1b seems to be closely associated with sacrifice. Bearing the decapitated head of a *cihuateotl*, Tlaltecuhtli 1b recalls the myth of Coatepec in which enemies of Huitzilopochtli, the sun, are defeated, their leader decapitated and dismembered. That Tlaltecuhtli 1b carries a personified blade in her mouth further emphasizes these connections to death and sacrifice. The headband that separates the *malinalli* hair of Tlaltecuhtli 1b from the rest of the head also recalls the red leather headband of the four-hundred Mimixcoa warriors. These warriors were sacrificed by Mixcoatl for the sun and earth and became a model for all subsequent human sacrifice (see Graulich 1988:395). The facial striping found on at least one Tlaltecuhtli 1b image (Figure 4d) may make these sacrificial associations even more explicit by marking the figure as "...the 'striped one,' the one doomed to the *sacrificio gladiatorio*" (Seler 1990-[III]:250). Klein interprets this striping as partial flaying, noting the striated portions of the face as being "...actually recessed as though the skin there had been removed" (1988:245). A third possibility is that this facial striping may be a reference to the earth as a consumer of filth, for, like Tlazolteotl, who is shown with a black-rimmed mouth, Tlaltecuhtli devoured garbage, excrement, and the dead, swallowing them back and then converting them into the elements of life. This eating of filth may also relate back to prisoner imagery, as prisoners are said to have eaten earth before their sacrifice (Durán 1994:327, 288).

Metaphors of sacrifice evoke the legend of the death of Tlaltecuhtli at the hands of Quetzalcoatl and Tezcatlipoca and her resultant request for blood and human sacrifice as reparation. Aguilera, for instance, notes that an open

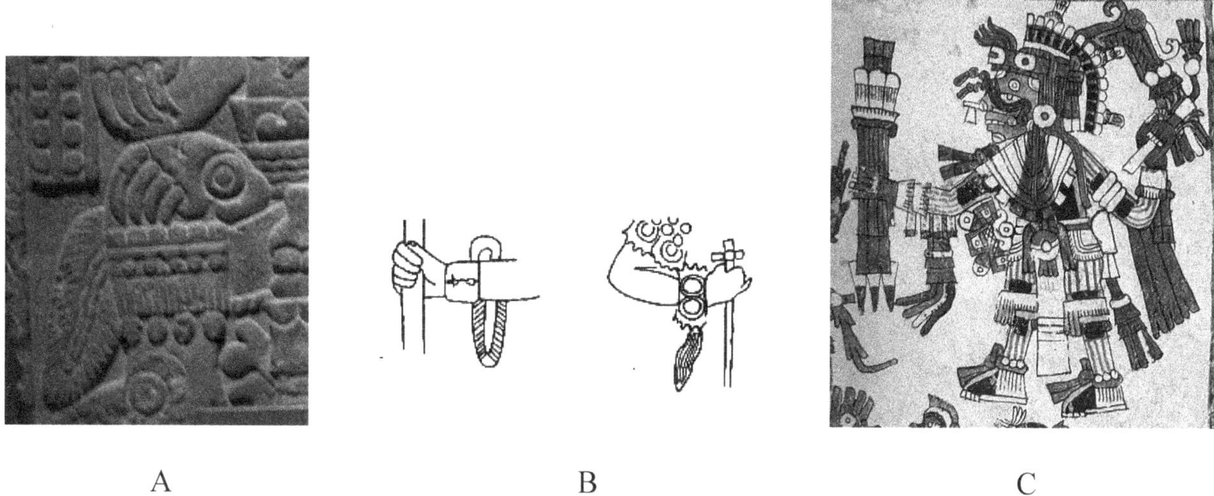

A B C

Figure 23: Coyote Tail Imagery; a) Tlaltecuhtli 1b (photo by author); b) Wrist-bands from Lintel 2, Piedras Negras and Stela 1, Lacanja (Stone 1989:f.10a,b); c) Codex Vaticanus B page 82 (possible coyote tails dangling from arm).

mouth, teeth, and tongue show a deity as a *teyollocuani* "Eater of hearts," "...a type of sorceress hungry to devour human hearts and drink their blood" (2001:14). Aquilera goes on, "The bare teeth mean desire to bite and the thrust-out tongue is a sign of thirst or being thirsty" (Ibid.:15; see also Aguilera 1978:46). Others describe protruding tongues and knives held in the mouth as symbols of death and the ends of life cycles (Klein 1976:204; Proskouriakoff 1968:248, Thompson 1960:78), an association consistent with Tlaltecuhtli's role as a great consumer of human sacrifice. Aguilera's (1978:46) argument that the protruding tongue is linked to sexuality also links the deity to procreation and production.

There are several attributes besides the female head that distinguish Tlaltecuhtli 1b from 1a. Several of these Tlaltecuhtli 1b images, for instance, like the 1a "knife variant," have double-outlined skulls lashed on to their forearms and lower legs. Again, this is a characteristic of Tlaltecuhtli 2 and will be discussed further on. Tlaltecuhtli 1b images also often hold skulls in their clawed hands and feet, perhaps a further allusion to decapitation and the use of the *tzompantli* rack for the heads of sacrificed deity impersonators. This characteristic is also shared with Tlaltecuhtli 2.

Shared Features of Dorsal Tlaltecuhtli 1a and 1b

There are two features that are shared by dorsal views of Tlaltecuhtli 1a and 1b that seem to connect these particular variants with warfare: tails attached to the legs and paper banners attached to the deity's wrists. The first of these are most likely representations of coyote tails, elements seen in the Maya area in imagery associated with Teotihuacan (Figure 23b). Coyote fur was an important element of warrior costumes at Teotihuacan, though coyote tails are rarely seen at the site (Stone 1989:156-157, 161). In Aztec art, these tails may have been shown on the wrists of deities (Figure 23c). Such coyote[15] tails are also seen at El Tajín, though they are shown attached to the bottoms of incense bags rather than associated with warrior regalia. A passage from Sahagún describing a dough effigy of Huitzilopochtli shows they may have been connected to this war god: "And his left arm band was hanging from his arm; it was composed of [strips of] coyote fur, and from it hung paper cut in strips" (1950-82[XII]:51). Stone (1989:161) discusses the coyote as associated with both the Chichimec roots of the Aztecs as well as warfare, for the coyote is a great hunter and, therefore, a great warrior.

That all of the dorsal Tlaltecuhtli 1a and 1b images exhibit paper banners tied onto their wrists further emphasizes this connection to warfare, particularly themes of capture and defeat. While in the case of Tlaltecuhtli 1a these banners are plain, those of Tlaltecuhtli 1b are spotted, possibly with rubber. In fact, the depiction of these banners is so consistent that a fragment of relief beneath a feathered serpent—which displays both skulls clutched in the feet and spotted paper banners—can be securely identified as belonging to the Tlaltecuhtli 1b category (Figure 5e). Sahagún connects spotted banners, called *amatetehuitl*, to themes of agriculture, stating that they helped "to produce the greenness, the growth and sprouting" of vegetation (Sahagún 1950-82:42). Generally speaking, however, paper banners are well known to have been associated with sacrifice, as they were used to adorn captured warriors and sacrificial victims before their deaths.

[15] Recent research by Nawa and Saburo Sugiyama (2007) suggests that these animals may be coyotes rather than wolves in the art of Teotihuacan." Bibliographic reference: Nawa Sugiyama and Saburo Sugiyama "From Dedication Burials to Murals: Re-Interpreting the Teotihuacan Animal Imagery" (Paper given at the 2007 conference of the Society for American Anthropology).

It is possible that these dorsal Tlaltecuhtli 1a and 1b images are particularly connected to themes of warfare and sacrifice. The four identical Tlaltecuhtli 1a reliefs along the edges of the "Stone of the Four Creations," for instance, show *atl-tlachinolli* signs emerging from either side of the deity (Figure 1e). The relief on the seat of the Teocalli of Moctezuma, also a dorsal Tlaltecuhtli 1a image, is similarly flanked by symbols of war, namely shields with darts and spears (Figure 1b). This may support Klein's (1988) contention that Tlaltecuhtli's splayed hocker body position shows defeat, for it seems that, at least in the case of dorsal 1a and 1b figures, sacrifice and defeat were emphasized over fertility and productivity.

Tlaltecuhtli 2

Tlaltecuhtli 2 (Figures 6-7), the male earth, is easily differentiated from Tlaltecuhtli 1, for the two forms only share three universal features: the hocker body position, two-dimensionality, and depictions in straight-on views. It is true, however, that several elements seen in certain Tlaltecuhtli 1 variants are also seen in Tlaltecuhtli 2 imagery. Tlaltecuhtli 2, for instance, clutches skulls in his hands, a feature already seen in Tlaltecuhtli 1b images. Tlaltecuhtli 2 also wears skulls lashed onto his arms and legs, a characteristic shared by the Tlaltecuhtli 1a "knife variant" and several Tlaltecuhtli 1b depictions. Though this feature is exhibited by some Tlaltecuhtli 1 images, the Gulf Coast style of the skulls indicates that they are really a feature of Tlaltecuhtli 2. Unlike Tlaltecuhtli 1, who is shown in both dorsal and frontal positions, Tlaltecuhtli 2 is only found in frontal views and, therefore, always faces the earth when found beneath objects. Unfortunately, as Tlaltecuhtli 2 was the variant most often reworked into Spanish Colonial forms—like millstones and column bases—the original context and placement of many of these carvings is unknown (Figures 7b,d,f).

Wearing a nose and eyebrow mask and displaying a mouthpiece with four conical teeth extending downwards from a gum, the face of Tlaltecuhtli 2 is upright, rather than in the position of decapitation shown by Tlaltecuhtli 1b. His headdress is formed of a horizontal rectangle with a triple dot motif inside. This rectangle is bordered by two crenellated elements that curve out and up on each side. Above the headdresses of two Tlaltecuhtli 2 depictions, the sign for "One Rabbit" is seen, a date that references the creation of the earth (Figures 6a,7c).[16]

Tlaltecuhtli 2 is obviously a male deity. He wears a typical male *maxtlatl* loincloth and displays no feminine features. In the middle of his body is a large feather-edged shield marked in the center with a quincunx, identical to the *kan* cross of the Maya. Projecting out from the sides and bottom of this shield are three pointed elements, possibly stiff feathers or spear-tips. His arms are shown with double outlines that curl inward at the elbows and armpits, and he wears undecorated wristlets and booties tied with a tassel. These booties have upturned toes and are marked at the heel with a cross. Tlaltecuhtli 2 also wears a necklace of double-outlined objects that bear a striking resemblance to the curling water or blood symbols described by Von Winning at Teotihuacan (1987[II]:8). Unlike Tlaltecuhtli 1 images, which display clawed hands and feet, the hands of Tlaltecuhtli 2 are shown with a taloned thumb only, while the rest of the fingers are shown in a naturalistic manner.

Features restricted to Tlaltecuhtli 2 imagery, including the figure's triple-dot headdress, facial ornaments, pointed boots, double-scroll arms, and a central shield marked with a quincunx all appear to connect the deity to the predecessors of the Aztecs, namely Teotihuacan, El Tajín, and possibly even the Maya. The headdress in particular connects Tlaltecuhtli 2 to representations of the Teotihuacan Storm God. The central shield and double outlines may also have prototypes at Teotihuacan. Though the ropey quality of Tlaltecuhtli 2 may associate it with the Teotihuacan net jaguar, it may also derive from Gulf Coast scrollwork and thereby links Tlaltecuhtli 2 to the site of El Tajín as well. Crouching figures at El Tajín, as well as Tajín imagery that depicts feathered shields and pointed boots underscore these possible Gulf Coast connections, relating Tlaltecuhtli 2 not only to the luxuriant vegetation and agricultural fertility of the area, but possibly to ballgame ritual as well. Strangely similar iconography from ballcourt markers at the Maya site of Tenam Rosario emphasize these associations, though how such similarities could have survived such spatial and temporal distances is unknown. Regardless, it appears that the iconography of Tlaltecuhtli 2 drew upon outside and preceding cultures for inspiration, and thus represents the Aztec visual interpretation of the old earth, the earth of their predecessors.

The Face of Tlaloc?

The similarity between the face of Tlaltecuhtli 2 and that of the Aztec rain god has led authors to call this earth deity "Tlalocoid" (Nicholson 1967, 1972), "Tlaloc-Tlaltecuhtli" (Baquedano and Orton 1990), "Tlaloc-as-Tlaltecuhtli" (Broda 1983:240), and, in some cases, has resulted in an unequivocal identification of the figure as "Tlaloc" himself (Klein 1973, 1976; Bonifaz Nuño 1986; Fox 1993). On the one hand, the headdress and mouthpiece can be linked to the Teotihuacan Storm God, generally accepted to have been the precursor of the Aztec Tlaloc. On the other hand, the diagnostic goggles of Tlaloc are missing from Tlaltecuhtli 2. It is true that he wears a mask over his eyes, but this mask curves over the brow without surrounding the eyes. Matos Moctezuma (1997:27) argues that this eye and nose mask is related to

[16] According to the *Leyenda de los Soles*, One Rabbit was also the year the sky was established (Bierhorst 1992: 144, 145). Not only associated with creation and beginnings, One Rabbit was also a year of drought (see Durán 1994:238) and famine. In the *Annals of Cuahtitlan*, for instance, it is said that "the people were one-rabbited," meaning they suffered a famine (Bierhorst 1992:103).

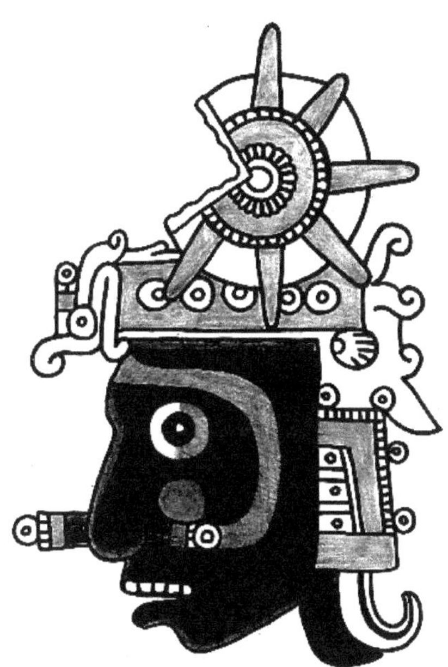

A

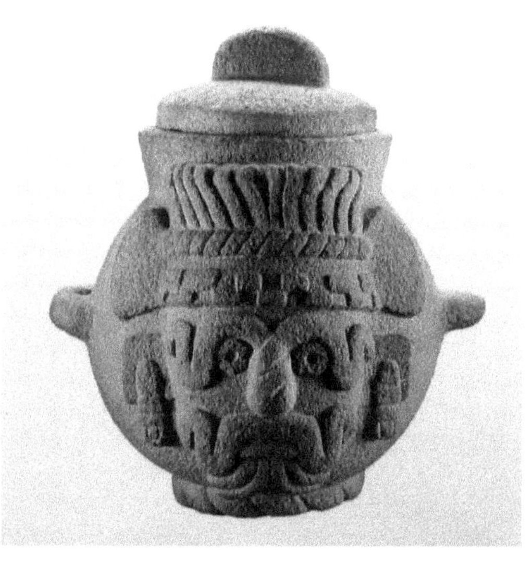

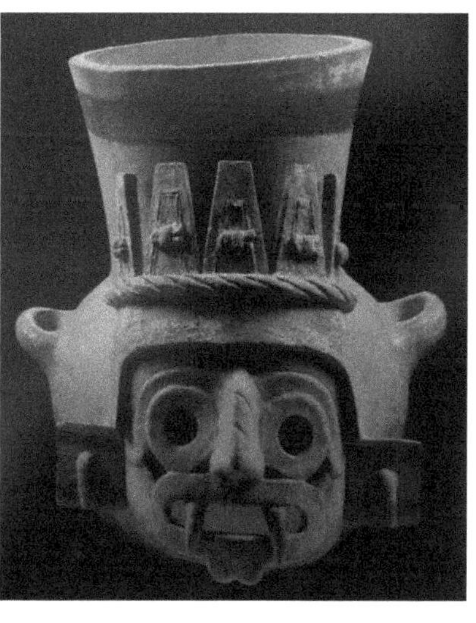

B C

Figure 24: The Face of Tlaloc? a) Face of Tonatiuh from Borgia page 40 (drawing by author); b) Lidded pot (Matos Moctezuma and Solís 2002:f.240); c) Aztec polychrome vase (Ibid.:f.238).

the curving brow ornament worn by Tonatiuh (Ibid.:30) (Figure 24a). Images of Tonatiuh, however, show this ornament as curving only over the eyes, whereas in the case of Tlaltecuhtli 2 it covers the nose as well. Though Aztec depictions of Tlaloc sometimes show a nosepiece attached to the goggles, this nosepiece is generally narrow and shown as two twisting strands, frequently depicted as intertwined serpents (Figures 24b-c).[17] The nosepiece of Tlaltecuhtli 2, on the other hand, is plain rather than twisted and the nose itself is shown as flat and broad with flaring nostrils.

These differences between the face-mask of Tlaltecuhtli 2 and Tlaloc are highly significant, for the two features used to identify Tlaloc in Mesoamerican iconography are his goggles and mouthpiece. At times, the goggles alone have been considered sufficient to identify figures as Tlaloc (see, for instance, Caso 1966, Bonifaz Nuño 1986, Fox 1993). That Tlaltecuhtli 2 lacks these goggles cannot, therefore, be dismissed as unimportant. Tlaltecuhtli also lacks the attributes listed by Caso as features of the Teotihuacan Storm God, including water torrents, clouds,

[17] Klein argues that this twisted serpent nosepiece of Tlaloc is related to the upright cruller of the Maya Jaguar God and the underworld sun (1976:82 f.n.2). However, the cruller of the Jaguar God always loops underneath the deity's eyes. Sullivan, for her part, sees this double serpent nosepiece as linking Tlaloc to Tlaltecuhtli by referencing the two serpents that once tore the earth goddess apart (1972:216).

jugs marked with the goggles and mouthpiece of the Storm God, shells, five-point stars, etc. (1966:254-249). In sum, though Tlaltecuhtli 2 does exhibit some of the features of Tlaloc and the Teotihuacan Storm God, they vary enough to render a straightforward "Tlaloc" identification problematic. It may instead be better to use the term "Tlalocoid" to describe Tlaltecuhtli 2, which suggests a connection to Tlaloc without equating the two deities. This terminology also avoids the issues inherent in calling Teotihuacan features (namely those of the Teotihuacan Storm God) by Aztec names. It is important to note, however, that I draw a strict distinction between the "Tlalocoid" features of Tlaltecuhtli 2 and those images that represent a direct combination of Tlaltecuhtli with Tlaloc (here referred to as "Tlaloc-Tlaltecuhtli" figures).

That Tlaltecuhtli 2 would wear certain features of the Teotihuacan Storm God and his successor, Tlaloc, is not surprising, for these deities appear to have been associated as much with the earth as with rain. Tlaloc, for instance, was associated with both the earth and the sky and was propitiated with rituals that took place both at mountains and lakes (Matos Moctezuma 1983:204). In fact, the identification of Tlaloc as a strictly celestial deity generally rests on a single image from Codex Vaticanus 3738 which shows Tlaloc as the ruler of the second layer of heaven (Klein 1976:80). Both Graulich (1997:124) and Caso (1970:61), however, note that Tlalocan in this Vaticanus image, located between the earth and sun, is by far closer to the former than the latter (see also Broda 1983:243 f.n.34). Tlaloc does appear to have often been more closely associated with terrestrial than celestial themes. In the *Historia de los Mexicanos por sus pinturas*, for instance, Tlaloc is called the god of the underworld (Garibay 1973:30).

Even rain, the special office of Tlaloc, was not necessarily a celestial concept, for clouds and rain were believed to be created inside hills and mountains, residences of the lesser *tlaloques* (Klein 1976:80 f.n.2; López Austín 1990:104; Heyden 1976:27). Similar terrestrial associations of rain gods are seen throughout Mesoamerica. For instance, the rain gods of the Yucatec Maya, Mixtecs, and Huastecs were all believed to live underground (Klein 1976:81; Redfield and Villa Rojas 1934:205,207). In the Maya area, caves were places of worship for both the rain and earth gods, and the lesser chaacs were believed to inhabit cenotes and caves. As Thompson states, "...the gift of rain is usually in the hands of mountain or earth gods" (1970:183). As a result, Tlaloc was more often associated with caves and the interior of the earth than the sky (see Sullivan 1972:216; Alcina Franch 1995:31). As Gillespie states, "Tlaloc was the master of celestial waters (rain) but his name refers to the earth (*tlalli*), and he was said to live under the earth..." (1989:88).

Tlaloc, more than a deity of rain or earth, was also seen by the Aztecs to be particularly closely associated with ancestral civilizations and was heavily utilized as a means of legitimizing Aztec rule. Pasztory states, for example, "... Tlaloc was thought by the Aztecs to be...one of the most significant patron or dynastic deities of the ancient civilizations of Central Mexico" (1988:289). One myth tells of Tlaloc welcoming Huitzilopochtli to Tenochtitlan as his son, indicating that Tlaloc may have "...functioned as a general owner of the earth who had to be propitiated by newcomers hoping to settle in the area" (Pasztory 1988:296). Tlaloc was also believed to have "...mediated actively in the transition from Toltec to Aztec hegemony" (Ibid.:297), a role evidenced by a myth in which the rain gods punish the greedy Toltecs by presenting them with jade and feathers in lieu of the "true" riches of rain and maize, causing four years of famine and the collapse of the Toltec civilization (Garibay 1973). As Pasztory explains: "In this myth, the transition from Toltec to Aztec rule is caused by the active intervention of Tlaloc who punishes the Toltecs and rewards the Mexica... it indicates very clearly that the Aztecs believed that Tlaloc was the most important deity of the earlier agricultural civilizations and that without his patronage civilized life could not exist" (1988:297). In light of this, it is not surprising that Tlaltecuhtli 2 imagery would owe so much to both Aztec Tlaloc and Teotihuacan Storm God symbolism. Not only does it link Tlaltecuhtli to both the rain and the earth, but indicates that this image may have served as a means of legitimizing Aztec hegemony by forging connections to the ancient rain god and the great preceding civilizations associated with him.

An understanding of Tlaloc relies heavily on the translation of his name, a topic often debated by scholars. Sullivan (1972) gives, by far, the most comprehensive and convincing linguistic analysis of the decipherment of Tlaloc's name, however, arguing that, "Strictly and grammatically speaking the name Tlaloc must be related to the adjective *tlallo* which means 'full of earth', 'covered with earth', 'made of earth', the plural of which is *tlalloque*, which also happens to be the plural of Tlaloc and the name for the multiple gods of rain" (Ibid.:215). Therefore, Sullivan determines that Tlaloc, above all, was an earth god: "Tlalloc means, 'he who has the quality of earth', 'he who is made of earth', 'he who is the embodiment of the earth'" (Ibid.:216). Consequently, Tlaloc should be understood as an earth deity, and the use of his attributes on the face of Tlaltecuhtli 2 should be understood as consistent with this terrestrial identification. As Sullivan states, "Surely, the mutual dependence of earth upon water and water upon earth in the cultivation of crops did not escape the Pre-Columbian farmer..." (1972:217).

It is clear that, lacking the goggles and certain other attributes of Tlaloc, Tlaltecuhtli 2 cannot be equated with this rain god, though the two should be understood as deities whose offices were deeply intertwined. The mouthpiece and headdress, for instance, connect Tlaltecuhtli 2 to the associations of Tlaloc and the Teotihuacan Storm God, including rain, fertility, and the

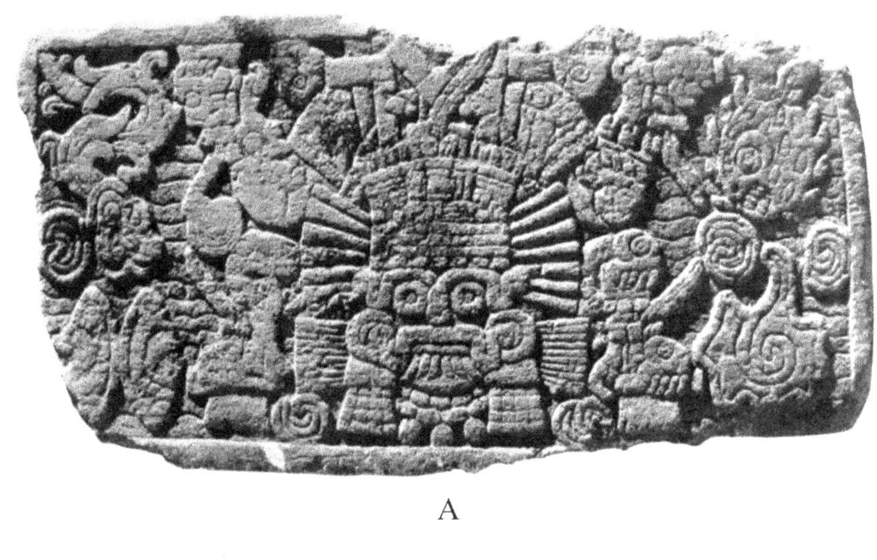

A

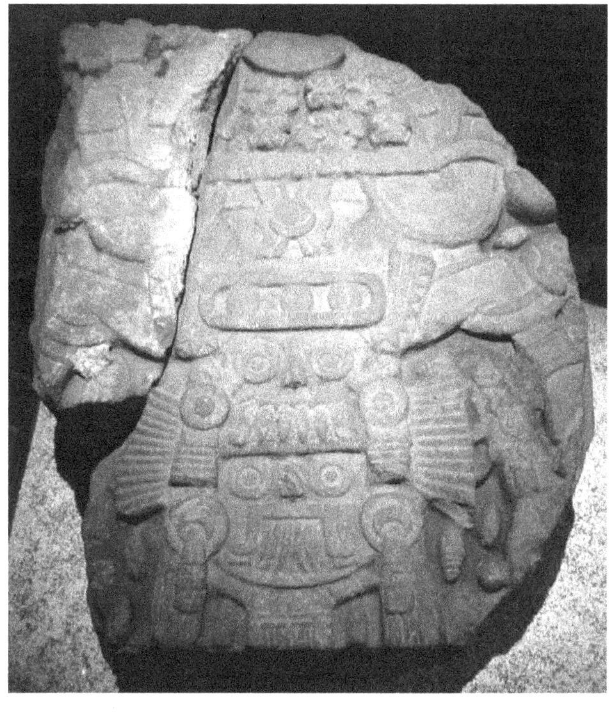

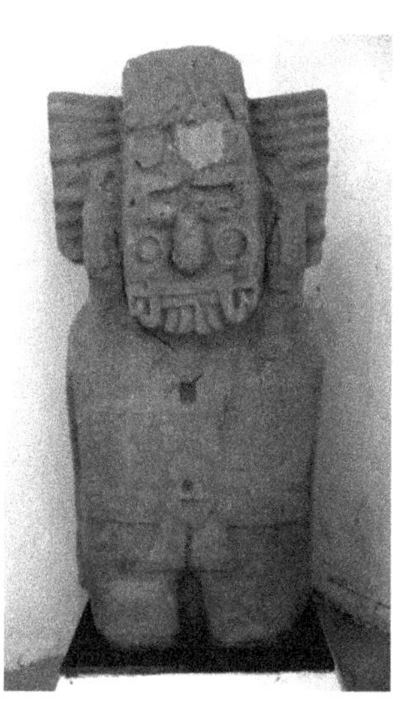

B C

Figure 25: Deity Variant Tlaloc-Tlaltecuhtli: a) Base of Chac Mool (Pasztory 1983:pl.140); b) Relief panel (photo by author); c) Statue from Castillo de Teayo (photo by author).

production of maize. Despite his close aquatic associations, though, Tlaloc was, above all, a terrestrial deity, connected to mountains and caves, his name translating as "he who is the embodiment of the earth" (Sullivan 1972:216). Interestingly, like sacrifices to Tlaltecuhtli, children sacrificed to Tlaloc did not have their hearts excised. Their throats were instead slit and they were afterwards put in boxes, thrown into water, or shut in caves (Motolinía 1970:34-35).

Tlaloc-Tlaltecuhtli: a Deity Variant

Two Tlaltecuhtli images show the earth wearing the true face of Tlaloc. One is found beneath the Chac Mool of the Templo Mayor (Figure 25a) and the other is a relief panel (Figure 25b). Such imagery not only stresses the important relationship between earth and water, but also highlights the difference between the face of Tlaltecuhtli 2 and that of Tlaloc. As there are only two images that show the direct combination of Tlaloc with Tlaltecuhtli, however, and as the two are not similar enough to be considered a clear category in and of themselves, they are here considered "Tlaloc-Tlaltecuhtli" deity variants rather than straightforward representations of Tlaltecuhtli.

The "Tlaloc-Tlaltecuhtli" image beneath the Chac Mool wears the twisted nose and brow element, the goggles, and curving teeth of Tlaloc, as well as the fanned paper headdress typically worn by Tlaloc in Aztec depictions. The body, on the other hand, appears to be that of Tlaltecuhtli 1a. With clawed hands and feet, jawed joints, and arm and leg cuffs edged with bells, this figure lacks the spotted banners and coyote tails typical of dorsal Tlaltecuhtli 1a and 1b images and does not hold skulls in its hands like Tlaltecuhtli 1b. The orientation of the head, however, which is upside-down, recalls the decapitated head of Tlaltecuhtli 1b. Since the skirt is seen wrapped tightly around the thighs, with angled edges, the image appears to be a dorsal view of Tlaltecuhtli 1. The background of this Chac Mool Tlaltecuhtli is formed of an assortment of sea creatures on a wavy ground.

The second image that combines Tlaltecuhtli and Tlaloc (Figure 25b) shows two bodies, one lying on top of the other, both with heads upside down in the posture of decapitation. The bottom figure displays typical Aztec Tlaloc attributes: a paper fan headdress, goggled eyes, and a curving, toothy mouthpiece. A small portion of a skirt with an angled hem is visible, marking this as a dorsal female body. Most striking, though, is the fact that the body of this Tlaloc is shown as water itself. Though only a small section of the left arm is visible, it is marked with waves and jade beads, representing, quite literally, a body of water.

The second figure, which lies on top of this Tlaloc water body, wears the same triple-dot headdress and crenellated elements as Tlaltecuhtli 2, thus referencing the Teotihuacan Storm God. Unlike Tlaltecuhtli 2, however, this figure also wears the goggles and mouthpiece of the Teotihuacan Storm God. The body itself, carved with double outlined arms and legs with skulls lashed onto them are also directly connected to Tlaltecuhtli 2 imagery. However, in this case, the figure is shown in an obviously frontal view, with a horizontal hemmed skirt, pendulous breasts, and a central *ollin* sign on the abdomen. The skirt is decorated with a skull and crossbones motif, which, along with the breasts, marks the body as female. The background of these layered figures contains spiral shells. Though an in depth study of Tlaltecuhtli deity variants such as these "Tlaloc-Tlaltecuhtli" images is beyond the scope of the current study, their remarkable iconographic complexity certainly merits further analysis (see Gutiérrez Solana 1990; Matos Moctezuma 1997; Baquedano 1988; Baquedano and Graulich 1993:164; Pasztory 1988:296).

Connections to Teotihuacan

Several of the features of Tlaltecuhtli 2 can be directly linked to Teotihuacan. First among these is the triple-dot headdress with out-turned crenellated elements, a headdress that is identical to that worn by the variant of the Teotihuacan Storm God that Von Winning describes as "Lightning Tlaloc" (1987[I]:68) (Figure 26a). Several non-Storm God figures are shown with this headdress at Teotihuacan, however, which may indicate that it was used by the Aztecs as a general reference to Teotihuacan rather than a specific reference to the rain deity. The mouthpiece of Tlaltecuhtli 2 is also directly borrowed from Teotihuacan prototypes, though in many ways it bears more of a resemblance to the conical spider mouths of the Teotihuacan Spider Woman (Taube 1983) than to the longer, downward-curving teeth more typical of the Storm God. Whether mouthpiece of the Storm God or Spider Woman, this feature links Tlaltecuhtli 2 to themes of agricultural fertility and abundance, associations carried by both of these Teotihuacan deities. Taube also identifies the feathered rim of the shield born by Tlaltecuhtli 2 as a Teotihuacan-style mirror rim (1998:34; 1992), further linking this deity to Teotihuacan prototypes. Interestingly, shields marked with the attributes of the Storm God—a row of three dots above a quincunx cross and curling lip element—are seen throughout Teotihuacan, recalling the triple-dot headdress, mouthpiece, and shield worn by Tlaltecuhtli 2 (see Von Winning 1987[II]:65) (Figure 26b). Von Winning links the quincunx motif to jade and water, stating that, at Teotihuacan, it refers "...to terrestrial water, to water accumulated from rain " (1987[II]:11).

The feathered rim and internal quincunx of this central shield also bear a striking resemblance to the shield carried by a net jaguar in a Teotihuacan mural (Figure 26c), where the central *ollin* sign divides the interior space just as the quincunx does in the Tlaltecuhtli 2 shield. Nicholson describes the quincunx as a common *chalchihuitl* variant in Aztec art (1967:82). Just as the *ollin* sign is substituted for the *chalchihuitl* sign in one frontal view of Tlaltecuhtli 1a, the *ollin* and quincunx shields may both be related to ideas of the earth's center. Tlaltecuhtli 2, then, is most likely being shown in a frontal view, though connections of his quincunx shield to the back mirrors of Teotihuacan warriors may contradict this theory. The double outlining found on the arms of Tlaltecuhtli 2 further links the figure to the Teotihuacan net jaguar, who is shown as an entire being composed of intermeshed ropes (Figure 26d). Associations with the net jaguar do not necessarily contradict Tlaloc connections, for the two appear to have been related at Teotihuacan (Pasztory 1988:290). For instance, Covarrubias (1971) connects certain Tlaloc forms to the Olmec were-jaguar while Pasztory discusses Tlaloc B as the "Jaguar Tlaloc" (1974:15-16).

Though there may be a relationship between Tlaltecuhtli 2 and jaguar imagery from Teotihuacan, the headdress and mouthpiece of Tlaltecuhtli 2 associate the deity more with the crocodilian version of the Storm God, Pasztory's (1974) "Tlaloc A." One of the most important features supporting such a differentiation are that the lips of

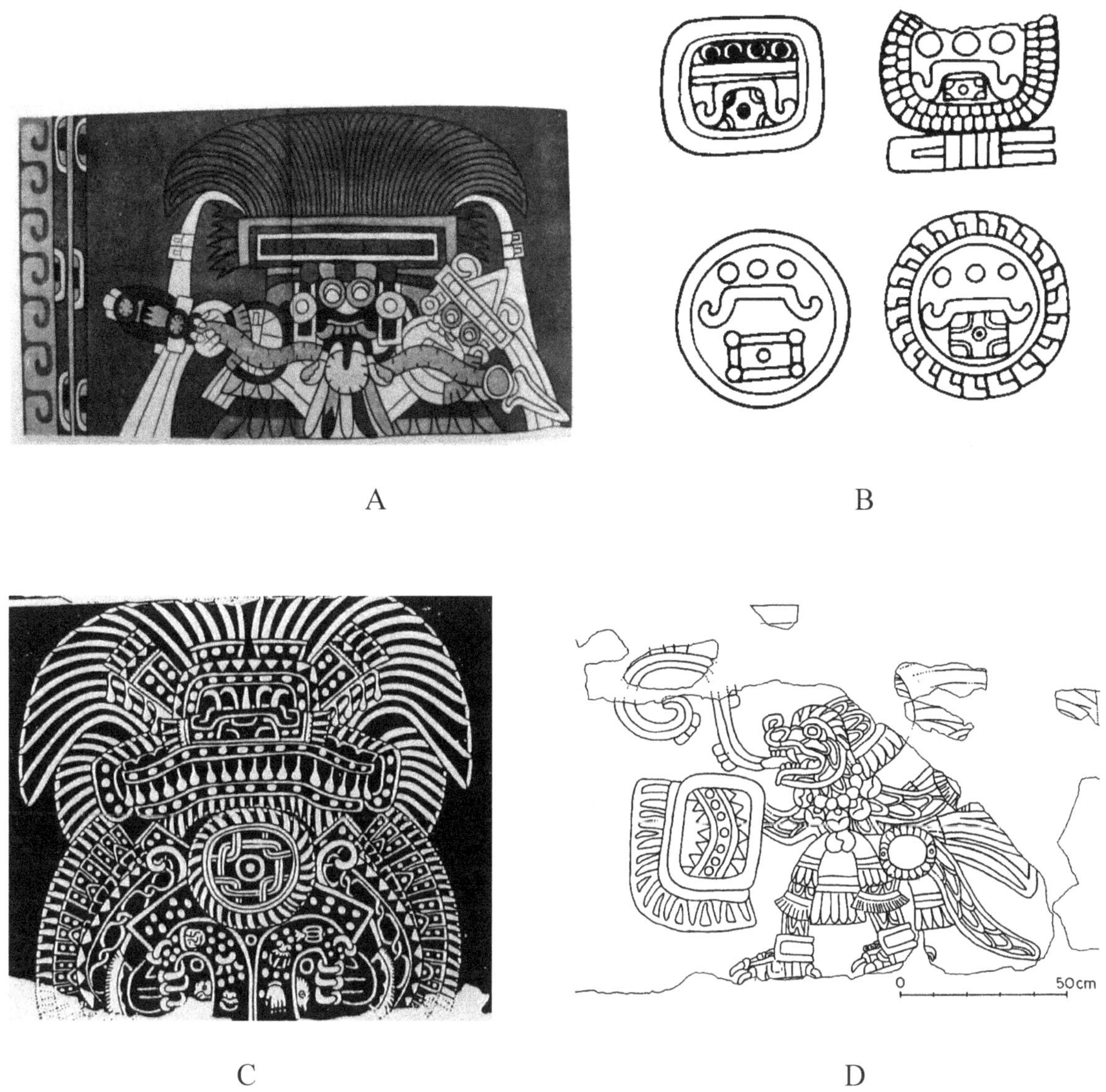

Figure 26: Teotihuacan Connections: a) Teotihuacan mural with Storm God (Pasztory 1997:f.2.1); b) Motifs from Teotihuacan (drawing by author after Caso 1966:f.3); c) Net jaguar with central *ollin* shield (Berlo 1988:f.12); d) Net Jaguar (drawing by Saburo Sugiyama from Paulinyi 2001:f.26).

Tlaltecuhtli 2 are consistently portrayed curling up at the corners, whereas Pasztory's "Tlaloc B" has feline lips that turn down (1974:17). The second factor supporting a crocodilian source for the Teotihuacan features exhibited by Tlaltecuhtli 2 is that he does not exhibit the forked tongue so characteristic of felines and jaguars in Teotihuacan art (Ibid.:18). The crocodile associations of Tlaltecuhtli 2 link him to *cipactli*, the great earth crocodile that floats on the surface of the sea. It should be mentioned, however, that Tlaltecuhtli 2 lacks many of the diagnostic features of "Tlaloc A," perhaps indicating that the Aztecs were conflating several Storm God types from Teotihuacan. With so much time having passed since the height of Teotihuacan, a more generic version of this Storm God would make sense, for the Aztecs may not have understood the differences among the different Storm God variants, details that only came to light in contemporary scholarship through the extensive iconographic analyses of such authors as Pasztory and Von Winning.

Like Tlaltecuhtli, Pasztory's "Tlaloc A" was a symbol of the earth itself, a fact demonstrated in imagery that shows trees sprouting from the deity's body. As Pasztory argues, this Teotihuacan deity was a god of both water and earth, which may explain why there is no known "earth deity" *per se* from Teotihuacan (Ibid.:19; see also Arnold 1999:43). This further stresses the problems inherent in labeling the Crocodilian Storm God of Teotihuacan "Tlaloc," for it appears that this ancient deity was a

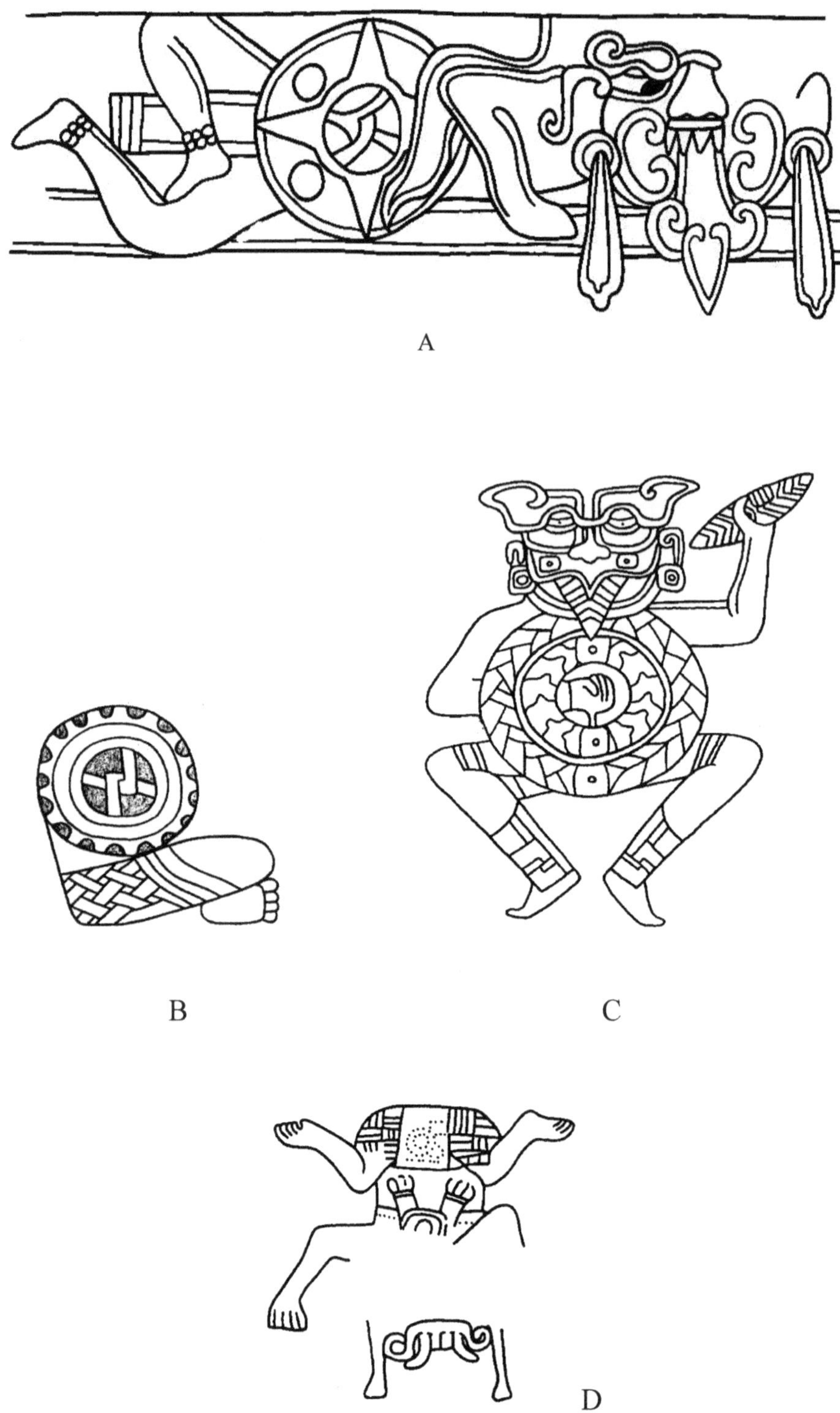

Figure 27: Gulf Coast Associations: a) Tajín sky god with central shield (drawing by author after Piña Chan and Peña 1999:112); b) Tajín shield with *ollin* sign (drawing by author after Kampen 1972:59); c) Tajín squatting god with pointed shoes and central shield (drawing by author after Piña Chan and Peña 1999:127); d) Descending Tajín god (drawing by author after Ibid.).

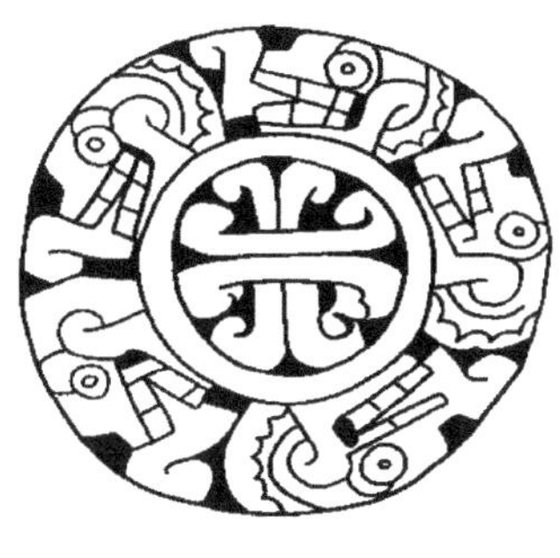

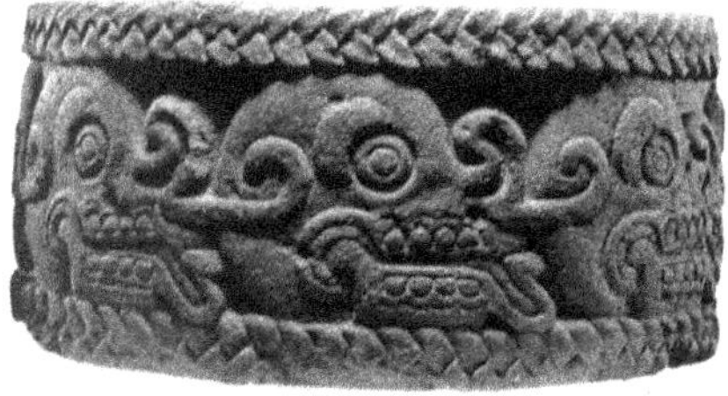

A B

Figure 28: More Gulf Coast Associations: a) Design on a shell gorget from the Huastec area (drawing by author after Beyer 1933:pl.11); b) Aztec *cuahxicalli* with Tajín -style skulls (Matos Moctezuma and Solís 2002:f.151)

combination of both earth and water, equivalent to a combination of the Aztec Tlaltecuhtli and Tlaloc. As Sullivan states, "...Tlaloc appears to be one with the earth, and it is possible that he was first conceived of as a dual god of earth and water and that his function as god of rain may have been a later development" (1972:217).

Connections to the Gulf Coast

Though iconography from Teotihuacan appears to strongly influence Tlaltecuhtli 2 imagery, the Gulf Coast is equally represented, particularly the culture of El Tajín. While the emulation and recollection of Teotihuacan is well known in Aztec art, a direct relationship with Gulf Coast prototypes is somewhat more unusual. Nevertheless, though his double outlined arms may connect Tlaltecuhtli 2 to the Teotihuacan net jaguar, the double outline itself is extremely characteristic of El Tajín art, where double scrollwork is considered a stylistic marker not only of the site, but of the Gulf Coast in general. Furthermore, shields with interlocked *ollin* elements are as numerous at El Tajín as they are at Teotihuacan. Several of these Tajín shield examples even show projecting elements or interlocked spears (Figures 27a-b), reminiscent of the points that project from the sides and bottom of the Tlaltecuhtli 2 quincunx shield. Shoes with upturned toes are also characteristic of El Tajín (Figure 27c), though the crosses on the heels of the booties worn by Tlaltecuhtli 2 are not known at the site.

Squatting figures in hocker-like positions, while absent from Teotihuacan imagery, are present throughout El Tajín art (see Fox 1993:58). Among others, three Tajín images in particular suggest that Aztec artists may have directly borrowed aspects of Gulf Coast styles to form Tlaltecuhtli 2. All three show supernatural figures in the hocker position while two of the figures display wide, flat noses (as do other images at the site) and curved brows (Figure 27d; see also Piña Chan and Peña 1999:123). With so much else borrowed from the art of El Tajín, it is more than possible that the brow and nose mask of Tlaltecuhtli 2 was meant to relate the figure to Gulf Coast cultures. A third image shows a deity in descent, wrapped in ropes and wearing not only the conical teeth of Tlaltecuhtli 2 but a small central shield as well (Figure 27e).

Koontz identifies several figures at El Tajín as Tlaloc, connecting them to themes of death and creation. On the one hand, these figures are seen receiving the severed heads of sacrificial victims from the ballgame (Ibid.:74-75). On the other hand, they appear to be associated with creation themes as well. For instance, one scene from Ballcourt Panel 5 shows a squatting figure, identified by Koontz (1994) as Tlaloc, who performs penis auto-sacrifice over the bones of a prior creation (see Koontz 1994:76, 79-80; Wilkerson 1991:65). This scene may be linked to the *Leyenda de los Soles* myth of Quetzalcoatl letting blood over the ground bones of the previous creation (see Taube 1986:54-56). As a creator god, this Tajín figure was utilized in art as a means of legitimating rule, specifically through his presence in scenes of ritual accession (Koontz 1994:173), rites that, for the most part, were related to the ballgame, decapitation, and sacrifice. In this case, it appears that the El Tajín rain god may have served a similar function as the Aztec Tlaloc by lending legitimacy to those in power. According to Koontz, Tlaloc figures found in the iconography of El Tajín also indicate that creation was envisioned as a joining of the forces of earth and water, "...the mountain that raises the sky in preparation for the emergence of humans and the watery place where humanity is born" (Ibid.:83). As was found to be the case at Teotihuacan, the use of "Tlaloc" to identify Tajín deities is problematic, not only because the site predates the Aztecs by five hundred years, but also because residents were not necessarily Nahuatl speakers. Regardless, it is important to note that figures with the attributes similar to those of Tlaloc are associated at El Tajín particularly with scenes of death, creation, accession, and the ballgame.

The style of the skull ornaments lashed onto the arms and legs of Tlaltecuhtli 2 may also be derived from Gulf Coast forms. Shell gorgets from the Huastec area (Figure 28a), for instance, as well as Aztec pedestals and *cuauhxicalli* carved to emulate the Tajín sculptural style

(Figure 28b), demonstrate that skulls in this double-outlined form refer to the Gulf Coast. The only analogy to the wearing of these skulls on the forearms and legs of Tlaltecuhtli 2 that can be made at present are the kneepads worn by ballplayers (shown clearly in the Tajín ballcourt panels). In the Escuintla region of Guatemala, for instance, one often finds ballplayer kneepads in the shape of faces or skulls (see, for instance, Kerr #5103 and #8684). It is important to emphasize, however, that such imagery does not explain the presence of these skulls on the forearms of Tlaltecuhtli images. As such, this visual similarity is tenuous at best and requires further study. Another possibility, though equally tenuous, is that the tied skulls represent the bindings of prisoners, a theory that may better explain why Tlaltecuhtli 1 is also sometimes shown bound with skulls. Several other elements found in Tlaltecuhtli 2 imagery, however, do seem to connect the deity to the ballgame. El Tajín ballplayers, for instance, wear "...a plumed circle holding a pendant train of feathers at the rear of their waists" (Kampen 1972:47), an element analogous, though in no way identical, to the feathered shield in the center of the body of Tlaltecuhtli 2. The skulls held in the earth deity's hands may also refer to rites of decapitation so well known as the outcome of the ballgame.

Gulf Coast yokes, ceremonial objects that replicate ballplaying gear in stone, are themselves associated with the earth monster motif (Wilkerson 1991:56). As Tatiana Proskouriakoff describes: "Commonly this form is modified into a curious grotesque combining reptilian and feline features and thought to represent a mythological earth-monster" (1950:72; see also Furst 1972:37). According to Wilkerson, the earth monster carved on these yokes "...places the wearer symbolically in the 'underworld' or its entrance and, therefore, in a symbolic closeness to death" (1991:56, 1984:116; see also Gillespie 1991:338). Though Proskouriakoff describes these yokes as part of the "Classic Veracruz" style and distinct from El Tajín (1950), the connection between the ballgame and representations of the earth nonetheless appears to be a characteristic theme of Gulf Coast art.

Though El Tajín is not generally emphasized as a direct source of Aztec borrowing, the image of Tlaltecuhtli 2 demonstrates a high degree of emulation of Gulf Coast styles. Though the full meaning of these stylistic and iconographic influences are unknown at this time, the Gulf Coast was known as a green and fertile place, associated with the coming of the rains and the fertilizing wind breath of Quetzalcoatl. Of particular note here is a Tlaltecuhtli variant from the Huastec area, which shows Quetzalcoatl in the hocker position with the clawed hands of Tlaltecuhtli (Figure 29). The appearance of Tajín imagery in representations of Tlaltecuhtli 2, like that of the Teotihuacan Storm God, might therefore allude to themes of rain and agricultural abundance. Connections to El Tajín also associate Tlaltecuhtli 2 specifically with the ballgame, a ritual complex so important in the imagery of the Gulf Coast and linked to themes of agricultural renewal and the repayment of blood debt to the gods.

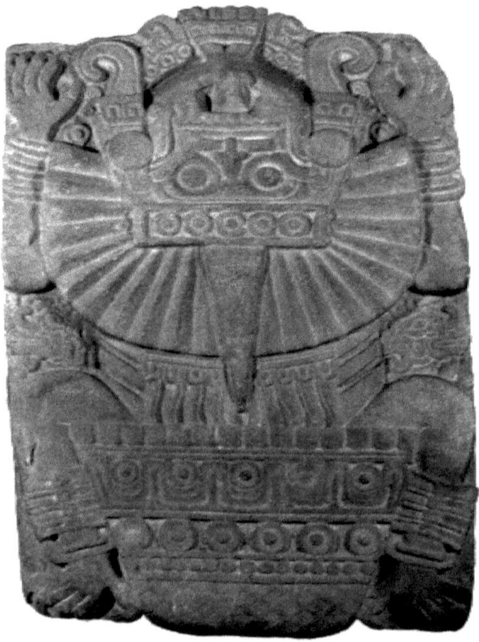

Figure 29: Quetzalcoatl-Tlaltecuhtli relief from the Huastec Area (Solís 1998:f.171).

The Aztec Earth and the Ballgame

That the earth and the ballgame were closely related is substantiated by Aztec myth. The ballcourt itself was considered a microcosm of the universe, in which the daily cycle of the sun as well as the changes of the seasons were replayed and confirmed. As Graulich states, "In this game the passage of the ball from one side to the other was supposed to secure the alternation of the seasons" (1988:402; see also Baquedano and Graulich 1993:168). Seasonal change was also a feature of the relationship between the earth and the sun; the former was connected to agriculture and the rainy season, while the latter was connected to the dry season and warfare.

These themes come together in the migration myth of the Aztecs, in which Huitzilopochtli kills Coyolxauhqui at Coatepec, slitting her throat and excising her heart over the center of the ballcourt at midnight, an act which makes the water, vegetation, and animals disappear (Durán 1994:27). This event symbolizes the defeat of the terrestrial rainy season by the solar dry season (Baquedano and Graulich 1993:168) as well as the triumph of day over night. As Huitzilopochtli's first actions at Coatepec include both the creation of a ballcourt as well as the erection of a *tzompantli*, one might infer that Coyolxauhqui was decapitated rather than simply having her throat slit. Therefore, this myth may celebrate the first Aztec double immolation, the first sacrifice given to both the earth and sun. Decapitation, characteristic of sacrifices to the earth, is well known to have been associated with ballgame ritual, and is

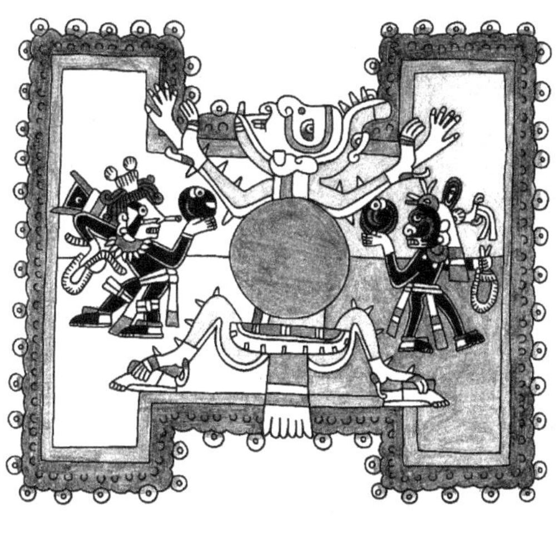

A

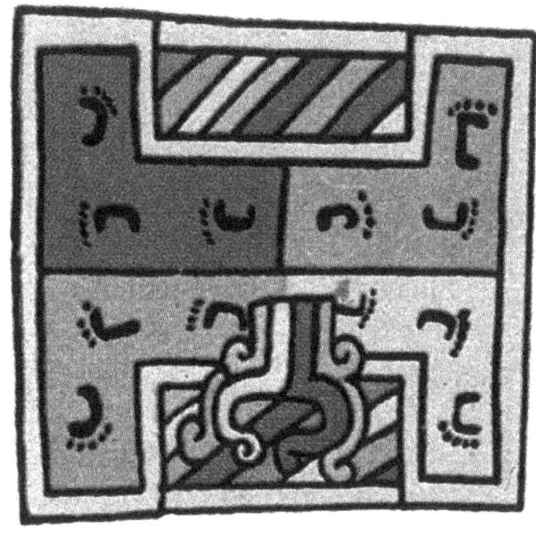

B

Figure 30: The Earth and the Ballgame: a) Figure dressed in *cipactli* skin over ballcourt (drawing by author after Díaz and Rodgers 1993:pl.35); b) Ballcourt divided into four quadrants (Nuttall 1975:2).

explicitly referenced in imagery from El Tajín. The association between the ballgame, decapitation, and agricultural fertility is similarly referenced in imagery that depicts decapitated ballplayers with snakes and plants sprouting from their necks (Baquedano and Graulich 1993:167-168; Hellmuth 1975:16 pl.8, 17 pl.9; 1978:80).

Scenes from the Borgia Codex visually express the conflation of the ballcourt with the body of the earth. On Borgia page 35 (Figure 30a), for instance, a figure dressed in the skin of *cipactli*, the crocodilian earth, is shown with his four limbs in the hocker position, spread to the four corners of the ballcourt. The center of the figure is marked as a large red circle, perhaps a conflation of the rubber ball and the great earth opening, the entryway to Mictlan, that was believed to mark the center of the field. This underworld realm was also called *tlaxicco*, "the navel of the earth" (Klein 1973:71). Gillespie discusses the four-quartered ballcourt and the four-limbed human body as metaphors for the quadrapartite division of the world (1991:336-337) (Figure 30b), while Seler states, "The earth, stretching in all directions, was divided into special sectors, just like the ball ground" (1990-[V]:7). Though the hocker position present in all Tlaltecuhtli imagery designates the earth body as organized into four quarters, Tlaltecuhtli 2 figures particularly emphasize this theme. The central shield with its quincunx and the small crosses on the booties mark the deity as representing the four quarters of the world as well as its center.[18] It should be noted, however, that this quincunx not only refers to spatial concepts but time as well. Since "...the kan cross itself signified the 365 day solar cycle and the concept of completed time..." (Klein 1976:196, 1980:180), it marks the body of Tlaltecuhtli 2 as the place of beginnings and endings, the center of both time and space.

Ballcourt markers from the Maya site of Tenam Rosario (a site in Chiapas, Mexico), which show ballplayers in the squatting hocker position, may further support this connection of Tlaltecuhtli 2 to the ballgame (Figure 31). How such imagery could have been transmitted across such time and space, however, is unknown. Fox (1993) identifies these Tenam Rosario figures as ballplayers. They do appear to wear the thickly padded waistbands seen in ballgame imagery throughout the Maya area, and all of them wear what might be *palmas*, one shown as a frontal skull. As the ballgame was considered ritual warfare, the reenactment of the sun's battles in the underworld, it is not surprising that these ballplayers are shown with the attributes of warriors as well. Stone, for instance, describes the Tenam Rosario figures as wearing Teotihuacan warrior costumes, including *atl atl* darts, a shield and spear, "...rings around the eyes, furry wrist and ankle bands with pendant furlike elements, a nose bar, and the scroll-jawed Tlaloc mask..." (Stone 1989:165). It must be remembered that the goggles worn by figures in Maya art, though often viewed as Tlaloc identifiers, are frequently markers of warrior status instead. As the figures at Tenam Rosario seem to blend the paraphernalia of the ballgame with the regalia of war, they suggest that Tlaltecuhtli 2 imagery may have been connected to similar themes.

Another intriguing detail of the Tenam Rosario figures is that they show projecting elements similar to those found on the central *kan* shield of Tlaltecuhtli 2, though it

[18] This directionality is also a quality of Tlaloc who, as Sullivan explains "...had a five-fold nature and he was conceived as sitting in the center of the courtyard of his four-sided domain directing the work of those extensions of himself called the Tlaloque" (Sullivan 1972:213).

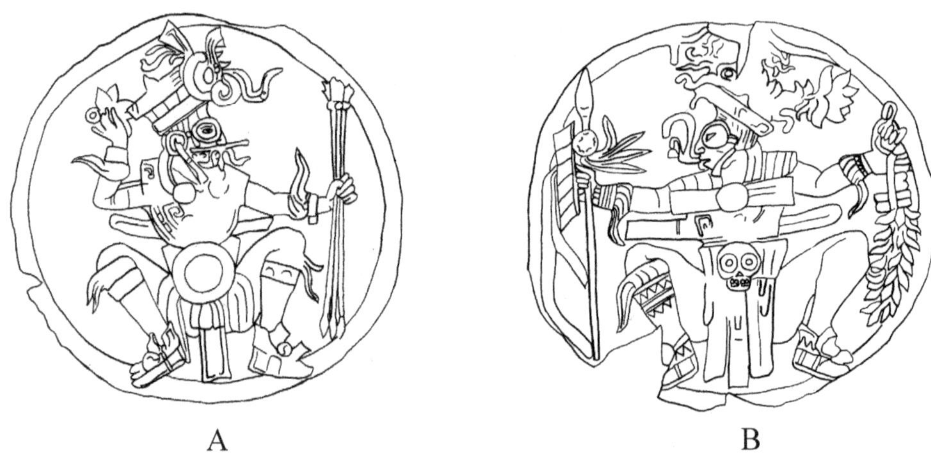

Figure 31: Maya Connections: a-b) Ballcourt markers 2 and 1 from Tenam Rosario (Fox 1993:f.3, f.2).

should be mentioned that, while the Tenam Rosario figures show two horizontal elements, Tlaltecuhtli 2 shows three, one projecting downward. Klein (1980:162) argues that these horizontal projections, when found on Tlaltecuhtli 2, are breasts, designating Tlaltecuhtli 2 as ambiguously-sexed. Such an identification, however, seems implausible, not only because there are three of them, but because, rather than being modeled with the roundness of breasts, they are pointed and bifurcated lengthwise by an incised line. It is possible that they instead are flints or spears, though the format is unconventional. They may also be feathers, especially as they have the same bifurcated style as is commonly used in feather depictions. Unlike standard portrayals of feathers, however, they are shown as though they are stiff rather than flexible. A mural from the Gulf Coast site of Las Higueras that depicts a squatting figure bearing a central shield bordered by four solar ray symbols (Gendrop 1971:f.123), provides yet another alternative for the shield of Tlaltecuhtli 2. This suggests that Tlaltecuhtli 2 imagery may even have been drawn from the Huastec area. Such iconographic sharing, clearly evidenced by the Aztec adoption of Huastec deities like Tlazolteotl, is further established by the aforementioned Huastec stone relief that bears a combined Quetzalcoatl-Tlaltecuhtli image (Figure 29).

Part IV: Discussion and Conclusion

The Implications of Gender Division

Now that we have determined that there were two different Aztec earths, and because the primary quality that governs their division is gender, it appears necessary to, at least briefly, address the implications this imagery may have for our understanding of gender relationships in Aztec society. In other words, does this iconography indicate that we need to reassess our conceptions about the principles and stereotypes of masculine and feminine in the Aztec world? Such a discussion is indeed important and, by all means, can and should extend beyond the summary thoughts expressed below. In all, Tlaltecuhtli imagery presents an extremely complex picture of female and male categories and indicates that discussions of gender may need to become more nuanced, and notions of what it means to be "male" or "female" may need to be reexamined if we are to hope to understand Aztec gender structures better.

Currently, there is much disagreement among scholars as to the exact nature of gender constructions in the Aztec world. Brumfiel summarizes the nature of this debate, "The debate centers upon whether Aztec gender relations were hierarchical or complementary and whether Aztec women accepted an ideology of male dominance or vigorously contested it" (1996:144). There are two primary theories on Aztec gender constructions. The first holds females in Aztec society to have been subjugated, dominated, stripped of power, and relegated to the domestic realm (see Nash 1978; Rodríguez 1988; Brumfiel 1996; Klein 1988,1993,1994,etc.). The second, in contrast, argues that Aztec women actually wielded a certain amount of political, economic, and ideological power, despite stories of their subjugation by the male-dominated state. In other words, this side holds that female and male gender roles were parallel and complementary structures and that such parallelism indicates that women not only performed functions crucial to the state, but wielded power and influence that was recognized by the general populace (McCafferty and McCafferty 1988, 1991; Kellogg 1988; Joyce 2000).

At first glance, Tlaltecuhtli 1 imagery appears to support the first school of thought. Splayed like the skinds of sacrificial victims, wearing sacrificial banners, wearing and carrying skulls, and even shown decapitated at times, this earth does appear to support. Klein's (1988, 1993, 1994) arguments about images of defeated warrior women as cautionary tales against challenging the state. In this case, Tlaltecuhtli would represent what Klein calls the "enemy woman" in Aztec thought, those females who signify threats "...to the power and legitimacy of the state itself" (Klein 1994:225) and are thus destroyed, usually in a pointedly violent manner. Here, then, Tlaltecuhtli 1 appears to provide further iconographic evidence for Aztec women as a subjugated class. As a state-sponsored image, she seems to express the imperial ideology of male dominance and control over women, a common theme of Aztec monumental sculpture (see Brumfiel 1996:155-57). As Brumfiel argues, in Aztec monumental works such as the famous "Coatlique" and Coyolxauhqui stone, "...images of mutilated women represent the Aztec state's subjugation of its enemies... These sculptures also seem to condone the use of physical violence against women to achieve male goals" (1996:156-157, citing Klein 1988 and Rodríguez 1988:126).

It is true that one cannot draw a one-to-one correspondence between gender constructions in real life and those illustrated for supernatural beings, but the predominance of images showing female deities violently dismembered, bound like captives, or with other symbols of sacrifice, does appear to indicate that such imagery, which carried messages of female defeat at the hands of males, served an imperial purpose. As Klein explains, even the story of Huitzilopochtli's birth at Coatepec was a gendered metaphor of the Aztec state: "The threat to Huitzilopochtli which was posed by his female relative therefore symbolized all pretensions—past and future—to Aztec supremacy. The conflict was expressed as gender opposition" (1994:226).

As will be discussed in the next section, the iconographic division between Tlaltecuhtli 1 and 2 forms appears to be a result of an Aztec effort to portray both the old, ancestral earth (Tlaltecuhtli 2) as well as the new, warlike earth of the Mexica (Tlalecuhtli 1). That the new earth, the Mexica earth, was a female marked with imagery of war and sacrifice is certainly interesting, especially when compared to the male ancestral earth, who, though wearing a war shield and carrying skulls, is far less explicitly violent in his iconography. The advent of the new female earth as the Aztecs began their empire building seems to maintain theories that such violent female imagery was a Mexica introduction. In other words, this new, sacrificed, bloody female earth might represent a new gender ideology that placed women in roles more subordinate than preceding cultures had. This could be used to support arguments that hold the advent of the Aztec Empire as the beginning of the demise of female power. Nash, for instance, states, "Terminological reference to females at the highest levels, although the posts were occupied by men, suggests that women may have played leading political roles before the state was centralized" (1978:353). This is to say, as the Aztecs expanded their empire, they replaced an ideology of gender balance with one of gender hierarchy. "The principle of complementarity between the sexes seemed to be dying out as sex antagonism grew in the course of conquest" (Ibid.:359). As a result, one sees in the Aztec Empire what Nash calls a "constant diminution in the power of women" (Ibid.:350).

Some believe that this "diminution of power" eventually led to the ultimate, and almost complete, replacement of once-powerful female deities with violent male warrior deities (See Nash 1978; Brumfiel 1996:144). The belief in the balanced opposition of genders was transformed into an antagonistic relationship between the sexes, while female deities were demoted to secondary positions in the Aztec pantheon (Brumfiel 1996:144, Nash 1978). As Brumfiel states, "In Aztec hands, female deities became secondary figures: the spouses, concubines and subordinates of powerful male gods" (1996:145, citing Rodríguez:1988). Nash similarly argues: "Theological doctrines paralleled the structural changes in Aztec society. First, there was the emergence of a single god at the apex of a hierarchy of male gods, and second, the eclipse of female deities related to fertility, nourishment, and the agricultural complex" (Nash 1978:359). Certainly, Tlaltecuhtli 1, with her sacrificial banners, and especially the decapitated Tlaltecuhtli 1b, reinforces the view that once powerful female deities became bloodied and broken under Aztec rule.

Although Tlaltecuhtli 1 imagery does illustrate the increasing domination of women as the empire expanded, the critical role the female earth continued to play in Aztec cosmology and ritual indicates that female deities and feminine principles were not completely eclipsed during imperial expansion. As has been discussed, Tlaltecuhtli played a crucial and physical role in state sponsored rituals. For instance, she is present beneath some of the most visibly arresting and monumental sculptures in Tenochtitlan, not to mention in colossal form at the base of the Templo Mayor itself.[19] She was also carved beneath all-important *cuauhxicalli*, a constant presence during rituals of decapitation, heart extraction, and general prisoner sacrifice. Perhaps most importantly when speaking of gender relationships and power structures, however, she was both opposed to and conceived of as a complement to the male sun as the great receiver of human sacrifice. In light of this, it is difficult to argue that female deities were altogether forgotten and/or made secondary through the Aztec male-dominated state. In fact, the places where Tlaltecuhtli 1 was carved locate her at the head of the Aztec pantheon, equal to the all-important sun, Huitzilopochtli, and Tlaloc. She was everywhere at once, beneath everything, receiving everything. Far from indicating the earth's status as a concubine or subordinate, Tlaltecuhtli 1 images show instead how critical she was considered for the continuing function of the Aztec universe.

It is important to note here Joyce's (2000) argument that violent images and practices in the Aztec world were carried out with both males and females in mind. "Violence was central to Aztec state imagery, but it was not preferentially directed against women" (Joyce 2000:169). As Joyce explains, violence in the Aztec world, in both image and ceremony, was not selectively female. "Rather than manifesting an official attitude of deprecation of women the violence shown in these ceremonies, and recorded in the myths they dramatized, was integral to the Aztec state's promotion of an ideology of military dominance" (Joyce 2000:168). In this case, Tlaltecuhtli 1 imagery, which depicts the earth as both sacrificial victim and warrior, would not be a gendered statement of Aztec imperial control over and subjugation of women, but rather would act as an expression of a gender-neutral ideology of militarism, violence, and bloodshed. At first glance, it is true that both men and women were sacrificed in violent ways in state-sponsored ceremonies. It is also true that both male and female supernaturals exhibit violent imagery in Aztec sculptural works and that both men and women are the victims of violence in Aztec mythohistory. It also, however, seems clear that women are more predominantly depicted as the victims in Aztec history, myth, and iconography. It is not that men were *never* victims; it is simply a case of women being more often portrayed as such.

Despite arguments related to female subordination and relegation to the domestic realm, Aztec literary sources and iconography are filled with tales and images of women as potentially powerful and influential forces. For instance, historical documents, including law records, land ownership documents, and genealogies, testify to the fact that Aztec women did wield a certain amount of power in Aztec society. As Nash states, "At least by rough indices, women had equal rights in the law and in the economy" (1978:352). It also appears that the status of Aztec women had a direct impact on the status of their husbands and offspring, perhaps even determining their eligibility for certain political offices (Klein 1993:43,1994:228-229; Kellogg 1988). The influence that women often had over men is often expressed through their teasing, which could goad men into battle: "Thus the women could torment [young men] into war; thus they moved and provoked them; thus the women prodded them into battle. For we men said: 'Bloody, painful are the words of the women; bloody, heart-rending are the words of the women'" (Sahagún 1950-82[2]:62).

In Aztec mythohistory and iconography, females, female supernaturals, and female deities are often viewed as capable of wreaking extreme harm and havoc not only on mortals, but also on other supernaturals and deities. For instance, the tzitzimime pose a direct and dire threat to the sun as well as mankind (Klein 2000; Taube 1993). It is true that the power is often subversive and characterized by the dark arts, like bringing various ailments to male members of the family, the ability to perform sorcery and black magic, and using powers of seduction to capture and kill unwary victims (see Klein 2000:14 n.35, 1994; Rodríguez 1988:180). It is,

[19] See footnote 9.

nevertheless, power—power held and wielded by females. As a result, despite the fact that female deities are often shown in mutilated forms, one must balance ideas of these females as violated victims of the state against the fact that these females received such harsh treatment because they threatened to destroy the state and state-sponsored ideology. This is power. This is importance. Whereas the unimportant and powerless become invisible, those with power, or the potential of wielding power, become public. Therefore, these images of Tlaltecuhtli 1, like those of Coyolxauhqui at the base of the twin temples and the monstrous Coatlique, indicate that, while women may have been a dominated class, in monumental sculpture they were immortalized in their most powerful and threatening forms. Shown as decapitated, dismembered, and otherwise mutilated, they do demonstrate what happens to enemies of the state, but also (and significantly) imply that powerful things have to be destroyed in powerful ways.

In Aztec art, one is constantly confronted with "warrior women" (Klein 1988, 1993, 1994), both mortals and supernaturals who take up arms and participate in bloody battles. In the codices, for instance, one sees goddesses like Quilaztli bearing shields and weaving battens like warriors. Several authors see this as a negation of female power. As Brumfiel states, "[Aztec female deities] also assumed warlike elements of costume and character, indicating that no separate sphere of supernatural power was reserved to women, outside the male sphere of warfare and conquest" (1996:145, citing Rodríguez:1988). Brumfiel (1996:157) acknowledges the argument that such imagery represents gender parallelism by marking female deities as equally powerful as male deities (see McCafferty and McCafferty 1988), but believes that these images of goddesses bearing shields and "phallic staffs" do exactly the opposite. Citing Yólotl González (1979:17) and María Rodríguez (1988:182-83), Brumfiel argues that "...such images are androgynous negations of a power grounded in femaleness. Rather than affirming an equivalence of male and female power, these images suggest that power can be obtained only through maleness. Androgynous goddesses are an artistic solution to the conceptual problem of representing powerful females under the prevailing ideology of male dominance" (1996:157). Such an argument holds that women cannot be powerful in their own terms, but must rely on the adoption of male features to exert authority.

Although such an argument is certainly valid, there are several issues that I believe need to be acknowledged. First, as Klein (1993) has shown, shields in the Aztec world were conceived of as metaphors of the female body. The carrying of shields by female deities, therefore, cannot be argued to indicate the adoption of male symbolism. Second, though staffs can be easily argued to be phallic symbols, in many cases these warrior goddesses are shown holding weaving battens instead, which, despite potential phallic undertones, are quintessentially female implements. Lastly, I think it is important to question the general assumption that warfare was not only a categorically male pastime, but that its associations were equally and absolutely male. As Nash cites, Toltec women, the preferred wives of Aztec leaders, were often active participants in war (1978:353). One must also acknowledge that women constantly participated in metaphorical warfare through childbirth. As Joyce states, "In the service of [imperial] ideology, both men and women were encouraged to think of themselves as warriors for the state, engaged in complementary actions that supported the expansion of the Mexica domain" (2000:169). Male warriors also appear to have borne objects highly symbolic of women into battle. Shields were one such object (Klein 1993), but these men also sought out body parts (the middle finger or hair in particular) of women dead in their first childbirth to make them stronger in war (see Klein 1993:47. In sum, the argument that female deities have been denied their own form of authority by being forced to accept male symbols of power relies on two major assumptions: first, that these symbols are, in fact, male; and second, that being a warrior and warfare itself were categorically and absolute male structures.

In Western societies, warfare has generally been understood as a typically male activity. So, too, it appears that Aztec warfare was decidedly masculine in character. The Western viewpoint, however, may be responsible for essentializing and simplifying the issue, i.e. because these women are shown as warriors, they must be metaphorically male. Aztec iconography and literature, however, indicate that female characteristics and feminine associations were inextricably integrated into concepts of warfare. The idea of war and battle, then, may not be so completely male after all. In many ways, Aztec warfare was a synthesis of male and female, categories balanced against one another in a myriad of subtle ways. There is often a privileging of certain male allusions and associations of war, interpreting them as unidirectional, when, in fact they travel both ways. The most obvious of these is the fact that childbirth was seen as a metaphor for battle. It is just as valid and important, however, that battle was seen as a metaphor for childbirth. As is recorded in Sahagún, the relationship between captor and captive was interpreted in genealogical terms: the victorious warrior says of the captive "He is as my beloved son," while the captive replies "He is as my beloved father" (Sahagún 1950-82[II]:52-53). Issues like these, which illustrate the tendency to privilege or project Western conceptions of gendered activities on non-Western societies, highlight the need to reassess our assumptions about what was male and female in the Aztec world. We may find that we were right all along, but it is possible that some crucial characteristics of gender relationships, especially those that challenge our preconceived notions of what it means to be male and female, may have been overlooked.

The seeming ambiguity of earth imagery has often been seen as evidence of the Aztec integration of male and female into one, blended whole, a recollection of the primordial Ometeotl creator deity who combined female and male features in one being. The new understanding that the earth, in fact, had two clearly gendered forms, however, calls for the revision of this argument. Iconographically speaking, combining Tlaltecuhtli 1 and 2 imagery to make an ambiguously gendered earth would have been easy enough. It is important, then, that such a combination did not occur. Despite the need to preserve and disseminate these two images, the Aztecs, masters of synthesis and combination, kept them completely separate. Such division of form, I believe, indicates that these two earth images were held to be inherently incompatible; the male earth and the female earth were pure and isolated beings without the ability to merge. In light of the arguments presented above, it is difficult to argue that Aztec imagery ever truly blended genders to the point of their becoming indeterminate. It is, in fact, probable that such ambiguous configurations would have been viewed as unnatural, because the dichotomy of the sexes precluded any potential of their becoming indistinguishable in a blended form. It is true that females are shown with male symbols and vice versa, but the importance of this overlap lies in their contrasting significance, the balanced opposition of gender roles, not in their unification or amalgamation. Male and female were always disparate categories in the Aztec world, which means that gender combinations must have been carried out extremely conscientiously in art and iconography.

Here it is important to discuss Joyce's arguments against dichotomy as an applicable model for Aztec gender relations. As she states "...the assumption of fixed dichotomous genders grounded in absolute distinctions in biology is a commonplace of the modern western European intellectual tradition. There is no reason to assume that this was a feature of other societies and other times" (Joyce 2000:6-7). Joyce's argument revolves around gender in the Aztec world as progressively and incrementally determined through performance (Ibid). Citing the presence of Ometeotl as an example of an ambiguously-gendered figure, she states, "...given an ideology of primordial gender dualism, the production of male and female adult genders is not something natural and inevitable; instead, it requires work to achieve adult gender status" (Ibid.:145). She goes on to describe gender in the Aztec world as "...something fluid that required work to stabilize" and argues that gendered performances actively shaped gender differences rather than merely reflecting them (Ibid:147). The shapes and definitions of gender throughout Mesoamerican societies, Joyce argues, were open to some variation and were not predestined as two absolute categories (Ibid.:150).

Though the Aztecs certainly did (consciously or un-) utilize gendered performance in both the domestic and public spheres, I believe such activities are best understood as reaffirmations of predetermined gender roles rather than creative processes of gender formation whose conclusions were open to variation. From the moment of birth, Aztec males and females were divided into strict and totalizing gender categories, and though it is more than possible that some individuals did not fit into these categories as neatly as hoped, the dual division of genders was the cultural ideal and goal. Therefore, the production and performance of gender must be understood to always (or ideally) have created the same two gender categories.

It is true that many Native American groups do view gender as a flexible category that is open to variation. The Zuni, for instance, address their children in gender-neutral terms until the age of five or six (Roscoe 1991:32,132). These groups, however, also have more than two categories of gender. There are females, males, men-women, women-men, etc. Despite the fluidity found in other New World cultures, however, and despite the fact that "...there are no terms to differentiate sex before the age of adolescence" in Nahuatl (López Austin 1988:285), it is clear that the Aztecs did not encourage this kind of gender flexibility. Alternative gender categories did not exist in the Aztec world. Of course, there is a difference between the actuation of gender and the cultural ideals of gender. In other words, there are always exceptions. Exceptions in the Aztec world, however (including transvestitism, homosexuality, etc.), were punished by death, indicating that, rather than negating the dichotomized framework of gender in the Aztec world, they instead act as exceptions that prove the rule. Consequently, I believe those figures viewed by some scholars as ambiguously gendered, like Ometeotl, are better termed "combined gender" figures. Rather than merging male and female into an indeterminate new gender category, these figures instead contain each of two separate genders. This combination of two oppositionally balanced categories emphasizes both the necessity of their division as well as their mutual dependence.

Despite my disagreement with some of her conclusions, Joyce's arguments do force a reexamination of our cultural assumptions and the ways in which these may affect our interpretations of gender in Precolumbian societies. In particular, she emphasizes the complexity of gender, especially in a non-Western context such as the Aztec world (Joyce 2000). Though I come to different conclusions, her efforts to reexamine the biases of both Colonial literature as well as contemporary Western scholarship is admirable. Gender in the Aztec world certainly was complex. Its complexity lies not only in the ways genders were combined, but in the basic definitions and associations given to each gender, which may contradict or disagree with those ascribed by Western minds. The combination of genders in single forms, including the wearing or bearing of masculine features by females and vice versa, does not indicate, however, that these categories were somehow fluid or flexible. Instead, it emphasizes that the Aztecs dealt with gender and gender definitions differently. The separation of male and female does not preclude the ability of a deity (Tlaltecuhtli, for instance) or a concept (warfare, for example) from exhibiting characteristics of both genders. It merely prevents or prohibits those genders from ever becoming indistinguishable.

It is clear that we need to reexamine, or perhaps merely become more aware of, the biases introduced by Western backgrounds, gender terminology, assumptions, and constructions. We must be very careful not to force Aztec gender relationships into frameworks determined by modern Western cultures. While such frameworks may roughly approximate Aztec gender systems, they are not well suited to eliciting nuance or subtlety from the record. Aztec society, iconography, and ideology were extremely complex, and we must resist the temptation to simplify something as complicated as gender relationships, a subject of much debate even in our own society. The Aztecs were masters at the blending of contrastive elements and meanings; they dealt with poetry in form and function; they combined concepts—like butterflies and warriors, birth and the capture of enemies—that would never be united in the Western world. Klein's work in particular emphasizes and illustrates the sometimes confusing, but often elegant, combination of these seemingly contrastive elements in the gendered Aztec world (1988, 1993, 1994, etc.).

It should therefore be understood that women may have been both subjugated and influential in Aztec society. They may have been considered enemies of the state as well as crucial participants in its success. Tlaltecuhtli imagery represents all of these contradictions, the powerful victim, the productive warrior, the mother and the enemy. Such combinations do not negate the differences between male and female constructs, but indicate that the relationship between them requires self-conscious discussion. As Kellogg states, "...it seems inadequate to employ terms such as 'equal' or 'subordinate' to describe the role of women in the Aztec religious system—in other words, to impose western standards or categories onto the Aztec religious realm" (1988:676).

It should be understood that the arguments presented above are, by necessity, summary and cursory ones. The topic of gender in Aztec studies is multifaceted and complex and deserves far more space than is possible here. Though a broader and more detailed analysis is beyond the scope of the current study, these issues of gender relationships, Aztec imperial ideology, gendered iconography, and the role of gender in the formation and development of empire are all topics that merit intense analysis and attention. One of the hopes of the current work is that it will raise certain questions, encourage debate, and thereby serve as a jumping off point for these kinds of scholarly endeavors. Though I have mentioned certain implications of Tlaltecuhtli imagery, including what Tlatlecuhtli 1 imagery may tell us about gender hierarchy and relationships as well as what the strict division between the male and female earths might indicate in terms of gender dichotomy in the Aztec world, many further questions arise. For instance, does Tlaltecuhtli 2 and the existence of a male earth negate that which we take for granted to be female in the Aztec world? Can birth, production, fertility and nurturing be concepts that cross gender boundaries? An intense look at the male earth may cause us to further question our assumptions of what "male" and "female" meant in Aztec society and culture. Another question that appears, at least at present, to be impossible to address with any certainty is, in the case of those reliefs that were carved beneath sculptures and therefore invisible, whether it mattered to the viewer if there would be a Tlaltecuhtli 1or 2 beneath. Was there any ontological difference between the two?

Understanding gender is a key factor in "our understanding of state formation as a process" (Gailey 1985:78). As Gailey states, "...state and class formation *cannot be understood as processes without concomitantly analyzing the changing meanings associated with gender and the intricacies of women's changing status*" (Ibid. original emphasis). Gender relations, divisions, and conceived roles had a dynamic interaction with the development, expression, and maintenance of imperial ideology in the Aztec empire. The study of iconography may bring to light new ideas, contradictions, and concepts when dealing with gender in the Aztec world. More than a simple reflection of such realities, art and iconography must be understood as actively engaged not only in the maintenance of gender roles, but also as an active participant in the structuring of new gender hierarchies and associations. In other words, these images of Tlaltecuhtli, just as other imagery in the Aztec capital and beyond, were not epiphenomenal, passive reflections, but were instead integral to the expression and manipulation of gendered ideas through both time and space.

Reconciling Identities: the Two Faces of the Aztec Earth

The question remains: why develop two Tlaltecuhtli forms that are seemingly interchangeable, especially two forms that vary so extremely from one another? Tlaltecuhtli 1 and 2 variants occupy the same positions beneath the same sculptural forms. They are both only found in two-dimensional representations and they both depict figures in a straight-on view in the splayed hocker position. Details of the figures, however, including their facial markings and general attributes, make them completely distinct from one another. Those of Tlaltecuhtli 1 are drawn from Aztec sources and those of Tlaltecuhtli 2 are, for the most part derived from outside cultures. Why did the Aztecs view their earth in two such different ways?

The answer, I believe, lies in the multiple ethnic identity of the Aztecs. On the one hand they were conquerors, Chichimec invaders that believed they possessed the unique right to rule the Valley of Mexico and its surrounds. On the other hand, they legitimated their reign by forging ancestral connections to the great civilizations of the past. As Pasztory states, "On the one hand they glorified their status as outsiders and conquerors by means of the cult of the god Huitzilopochtli, on the other they sought to establish ties with the older local civilizations." (1988:289). Such battles of identity are not unknown in history. Even the Spanish in the New World fought, on the one hand, for independence from Spain by appropriating the unique cultural history of the indigenous population, and, on the other, for cultural dominance and control in Mexico by emphasizing their superior Spanish descent. If once sees the Aztecs as a cultural group struggling to reconcile the disparate parts of their personal identity, it is easy to see why a dual earth would have arisen in their cosmology. As Umberger explains, much of Aztec imperial ideology revolved around this contrast: "More important than the distinction between ancient and recent was that between Toltec and Chichimec, between things associated with the civilized and things associated with the uncivilized" (1996:86).

Tlaltecuhtli 1 recalls the Mexica past, the mythology of the migration south from their northern barbaric origins. The Mexica migration myth emphasizes the constant battle between male and female powers. Huitzilopochtli, avatar of the sun, kills Coyolxauhqui not once, but twice, at the hill of Coatepec, the first time at the moment of his birth from Coatlicue and the second time during the Mexica migration, eating her heart and decapitating her over the ballcourt at midnight. The Aztec civilization was thus born from a cosmic battle between male and female forces (see Klein 1988, 1993, 1994). This may explain the imagery of war seen on Tlaltecuhtli 1 images, the emphasis of Tlaltecuhtli 1b on decapitation and that of dorsal Tlaltecuhtli 1a and 1b images—with their paper banners and coyote tail wristlets—on themes of warfare and defeat. The coyote tail itself may have been envisioned as a link between the Aztecs and their Chichimec past, recalling the time when they dressed in the hides of animals, especially coyote fur, and survived through hunting, a practice considered analogous to warfare and the taking of captives. The insatiable Tlaltecuhtli 1a, with her jaws open to receive the blood of sacrifice and the bodies of the dead, may also have been utilized either in response to or in order to justify the increasing emphasis and reliance of the Aztec Empire on military expansion and human sacrifice.

Tlaltecuhtli 2, on the other hand, represents a male earth connected to the great civilizations that preceded the Aztecs. Teotihuacan, for example, is well known to have been a source of legitimacy for Aztec leaders as well as a source for religious iconography. The Aztecs also regarded it as the birthplace of the Fifth Sun. El Tajín was a precursor of the Aztec civilization as well, but its most important associations were to the ballgame, decapitation ritual, and the lush verdure of the Gulf Coast, origin point of the fertilizing breath-wind of Ehecatl-Quetzalcoatl. Connections to the Maya site of Tenam Rosario are more curious. Though the Aztecs had clear trade associations with the Yucatan Peninsula, direct influences from Classic period Guatemala are more difficult to prove or comprehend. An interesting fact to note is that little, if any, of Tlaltecuhtli 2 imagery can be connected to the site of Tula, so often referenced by the Aztecs in art. However, it must be remembered that the "Toltecs" for the Aztecs were any great and ancient civilization, and thus that the sites of Teotihuacan, El Tajín, and even the Maya area may have all been conceived as Toltec centers. As Pasztory explains, "By 'Toltec' the Mexica meant all the art of the past including both the Teotihuacan and Tula traditions" (1988:294; see also Umberger 1996:88-89)

Tlaltecuhtli 2, wearing the mouthpiece and headdress characteristic of the Teotihuacan Storm God, evokes the earth of the ancestors, before there was a separation between rain and earth, between Tlaloc and Tlaltecuhtli. The fact that "...Tlaloc was also a god of dynastic succession, an old god related to ancestors and to past cosmic ages or 'suns'" (Broda 1987:83) further highlights this link of Tlaltecuhtli 2 to ancestral powers. Interestingly, although Tlaltecuhtli 2 references the past and embodies the divine power of the old gods of earth and water, the form of this deity is not seen before the Late Postclassic reliefs of Tenochtitlan. In other words, Tlaltecuhtli 2 represents not a survival of old representations of the earth, but instead a new and purely Aztec interpretation of what the old earth may have looked like. As Umberger notes, these re-combinations and reinventions of ancient features were a commonplace of Aztec imperial iconography: "In their art, however, it is obvious that the Tenochca elite were re-creating within the city a conflation of different parts of the past, inventing a Toltec heritage in the broader sense" (1996:89).

Whatever his other connections, Tlaltecuhtli 2 should be understood as an old god, a god present at the beginnings of the world when the deities gathered at Teotihuacan and the Fifth Sun was born. Just as Huitzilopochtli, the new Mexica tribal god, was paired in the Templo Mayor with Tlaloc, derived from the old Teotihuacan Storm God, Tlaltecuhtli 1, the Mexica tribal earth, was paired with the primordial earth of Tlaltecuhtli 2.

The discovery that the Aztec earth had two faces reveals that the Aztec struggle to resolve the contradictions of a multiple ethnic identity were realized in very physical ways. Tlaltecuhtli imagery represents a delicate balancing act of past and present, of forging a new identity while at the same time incorporating the ways of the ancestors. Tlaltecuhtli 1 may thus be seen as more representative of subjugation, of the new emphasis on war and sacrifice and the pairing of the female earth with the solar patron

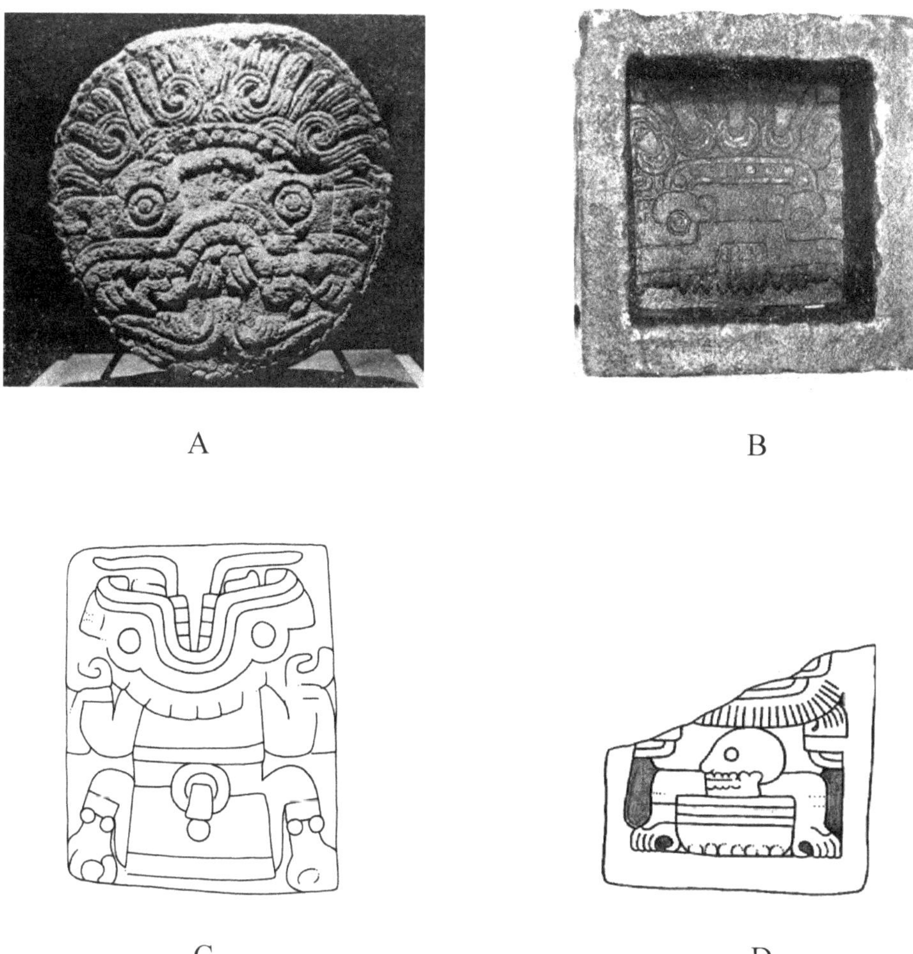

Figure 32: Some Tlaltecuhtli Variants; a) Tlaltecuhtli 1a head variant (Gutiérrez Solana 1983:f.68); b) Tlaltecuhtli 1a head variant (Ibid: f.22a); c) Relief panel (drawing by author after Ibid..:f.173); d) Relief panel fragment (Seler 1990-[IV]:232, f.47).

god of the Mexica, Huitzilopochtli. Tlaltecuhtli 2 may be seen as the other side of the equation, reflecting the dependence of the Aztecs on the civilizations of the past to legitimate their right to rule. As Pasztory states, "In these monuments the Mexica sought to express their emergence from a Toltec past and to validate their rule through symbols of artistic continuity" (1988:294).

The combination of two different earths in Aztec iconography also brings to light the insecurity of a cultural group attempting to forge a new empire. As Carrasco states in his discussion of the Templo Mayor, "Plagued by a sense of illegitimacy and cultural inferiority, the Aztecs made shrewd and strenuous efforts to encapsulate the sanctified traditions of the past into their shrine" (1987:150). Pasztory draws similar conclusions, "The Aztec rulers never totally banished the feeling that they were usurpers and that they had no legal right to what they possessed" (1988:289). Though they brought with them a new religious structure based on human sacrifice and extravagant public ceremonies, the Aztecs were not fully convinced that these new ways could justifiably replace the old, nor were they convinced that such total replacement would be a wise decision.

This inferiority complex may be witnessed in the lack of variety in Tlaltecuhtli 2 images when opposed to the greater variation of forms seen in Tlaltecuhtli 1. Despite its achievements, the Aztec Empire was still a fledgling civilization. Tlaltecuhtli reliefs capture the struggle of this new empire between preservation of the past in the prescribed form of Tlaltecuhtli 2 and the process of self-invention on the part of the Aztecs who, at the time of the Conquest, may still have been seeking the true face of their Mexica earth, Tlaltecuhtli 1. López Austín describes this identity crisis: "...the instability of Mexica dominion brought with it self-doubt as to the legitimacy of their claim to be heirs of the god Quetzalcoatl... the religious policy of the Mexicans seemed to vacillate between claiming to be Quetzalcoatl's sons and initiating a new era under the patronage of the god Huitzilopochtli. They decided on the latter option, but they themselves doubted up to the last moment the legitimacy of their rise to predominance" (1988:86). When the Spanish arrived, it was seen by the Aztecs as proof of their mistake in trying to forge a new empire governed by the god Huitzilopochtli (Ibid.). This loss of faith in the new religion may explain why Tlaltecuhtli 2, symbol of the old gods and preceding civilizations, is the Tlaltecuhtli variant that was most often reworked in Colonial times, preserved in millstones and column bases in a final, perhaps desperate, return to the ways of the past (Figures 7b,d,f).

Understanding the differences between these two Tlaltecuhtli variants diversifies our view of the Aztecs and generates a more nuanced view of the way in which the Aztecs envisioned not only their physical world, but their place in history. So often seen as warriors, conquerors, and the rulers of a great empire, the Aztecs are often assumed to have been confident, self-assured, and completely convinced of their right to reign over central Mexico and its environs. The pairing of their own Mexica earth with an image believed to represent the earth of the great preceding civilizations, however, indicates instead that the Aztecs were a people taking the first steps toward establishing their own identity. Because so much of what we hold to be Aztec culture and religion arose as a result of the adoption and adaptation of neighboring cultures' ideological and religious systems, it is often difficult to isolate forms and ideas that are purely Aztec. Fortunately, representations of Tlaltecuhtli— imagery never seen in other cultural contexts— provide a window into how these people, as newcomers and conquerors, struggled to understand their place in the world.

Summary and Conclusions

The earth played a critical role in the worldview of the Aztecs. Throughout sixteenth-century accounts of Aztec life and ritual, Tlaltecuhtli is described as a vital life force, a great consumer of human blood, and the representation of the order that arose—by violent means—from primordial chaos. The body of Tlaltecuhtli also represented the world center, the intersection of the four directional quadrants. The earth was not only the center of physical space, however, but also of life cycles. Because Tlaltecuhtli's dismemberment marked the world's foundation and because it was believed that earthquakes would proclaim its termination, this deity was also a symbol of the beginning and end of the current creation. "[O]n the day of judgment, the earth will turn over; the bottom side will be uppermost, and all present-day people will be destroyed" (López Austín 1988:246). Indeed, the end of the Fifth Sun by earthquakes was seen as the absolute end of all time, for the world would not be renewed: "In the Fifth Sun… the possibilities for creation were exhausted" (Ibid.:240). Tlaltecuhtli, then, not only combined the forces of production with those of destruction, but represented for the Aztecs the absolute center of space and time.

The Aztec earth was a duality, representing the crucial opposition and mutual dependence of male and female, life and death, production and destruction. Through close iconographic study, one can better understand the patterns behind Tlaltecuhtli representations by differentiating between that which is typical and that which is an exception. Typical representations of Tlaltecuhtli have been shown to share three features: straight-on depictions, two-dimensionality, and the hocker position. Study of the individual details of Tlaltecuhtli images shows that they are systematically distributed, adhering to strict rules that clearly distinguish two very different Tlaltecuhtli variants. Between the two forms, Tlaltecuhtli 1 shows much more internal variation, while Tlaltecuhtli 2 images vary so little that one wonders if a template was used in their making. It is through iconographic definition and the detailed analysis of which details comprise each Tlaltecuhtli variant that one determines the parameters of the imagery under study. These parameters exclude such images as head and crocodile variants (Figures 13b, 32) as well as Tlaltecuhtli deity variants, which include Tlalchitonatiuh (Figure 8), Tlaloc-Tlaltecuhtli figures (Figure 25a-b), a Quetzalcoatl-Tlaltecuhtli image from the Huastec area (Figure 29), and an Itzpapalotl-Tlaltecuhtli relief (Figure 12a).

The argument that Tlaltecuhtli is ambiguously gendered has been shown to be untenable. A close analysis of iconographic markers defines instead two earths, one male and one female, whose features, for the most part, are non-exchangeable. This fundamental duality of the earth is also seen in myth, where Tlaltecuhtli is designated as both a primordial victim of sacrifice and its great proponent. From the deity's dismembered body sprout all of the things necessary to support life, but in exchange Tlaltecuhtli cries out for blood and human sacrifice. In myth, then, the deity is seen both as the creator of life and the consumer of the dead. The duality of Tlaltecuhtli is also expressed in myth and ritual in the pairing of the earth with the sun.

Earth imagery, therefore, provides substantial support for the all-pervasive quality of the Aztec worldview in which opposites "…are conceived at the same time to be polar and complementary pairs, their elements interrelated by their opposition as contraries…" (López Austín 1988:52). Such tension between opposing forces gave sense and meaning to the Aztec universe by explaining "…its diversity, its order, and its movement" (Ibid.). Earth imagery, then, expresses and reinforces the fundamental duality by which the Aztecs structured their universe. This duality is clearly expressed not only in the oppositional pairing of sun and earth, but in the division of earth imagery into the female Tlaltecuhtli 1 and the male Tlaltecuhtli 2 variants, each of which encompasses themes of both life and death, creation and destruction.

The importance of the earth is further illustrated by the Templo Mayor, in whose form the Aztecs not only joined the dual forces of Tlaloc and Huitzilopochtli, agriculture and war, but also the triadic principle of water, sun, and earth. In this triadic structure, Tlaltecuhtli was, at once, the earth, the city of Tenochtitlan, and the platform of the Templo Mayor who received the blood and bodies of the victims thrown down the twin temple steps. As producer of agricultural abundance as well as a primary reason for war and ritual sacrifice, Tlaltecuhtli represented both the rainy and the dry seasons, both male and female, a fact that explains her place as the platform sustaining the temples of both Huitzilopochtli and Tlaloc.

The division of Tlaltecuhtli imagery into two forms (male and female) has been shown to have some important implications in terms of the ways in which gender may have been constructed and conceived in the Aztec world. For instance, the deity's division into two non-overlapping forms appears to support a dichotomy of gender in Aztec society. The features of this dichotomy, however, may need to be dealt with more carefully, as Western assumptions and biases may project essentialized gender roles on ideas and iconography that may have carried very different associations. In general, gendered imagery, especially that of Tlaltecuhtli, is extremely complex, and the multiple ways in which the Aztecs combined male and female features in iconography indicates that we may need to reexamine some of our preconceived notions of "male" and "female" structures in Aztec society.

The division of Tlaltecuhtli into two forms has also been shown to raise questions of Aztec personal identity, especially in terms of the ways in which the construction of personal identity intersected with the construction of political or imperial ideology. It is true that Tlaltecuhtli 1 reflects the Mexica preoccupation with war, sacrifice, and the addition and elevation of new deities into the central Mexican pantheon, but Tlaltecuhtli 2 reflects the equally important, almost obsessive, Aztec reliance on claims and inheritance from ancestral civilizations to legitimize their rule. As Umberger states, Aztec sculptural motifs revolve around several interrelated themes: "...the Tenochca's right to rule their world; their inheritance of this right from past civilizations, the cosmic purpose of the empire, mythical prototypes for Tenochca practices; and the defeat, humiliation, and lack of rights of the conquered. Even the styles and forms of monuments were significant; the Tenochca were very conscious of the art of other peoples and quoted foreign and ancient types for a variety of sociopolitical purposes" (1996:86).

Further discussion and scholarship are obviously needed to flesh out the implications of Tlaltecuhtli imagery. One relevant and important topic might be an attempt to reconstruct provenience information for these pieces. Though such data is lacking for the majority of sculptures, the creation of a rough chronological outline may be possible. Such an outline would help position these monuments in the history of the empire. Clarifying whether the two Tlaltecuhtli variations are, in fact, contemporaneous, or whether one form predates the other would change the entire tenor of the debate. Another area open to research might be the nature of visibility and invisibility in these often hidden Tlaltecuhtli reliefs, in other words, the ontological difference between the seen and the unseen both as political tools and as forums for the construction of both imperial and personal identity. It is hoped that the current study can be utilized as a solid basis for these kinds of studies. Much work remains before we can truly understand the ways in which the Aztecs positioned themselves *vis á vis* the face of the earth.

In sum, the current study shows that an understanding not only of the broader features of Aztec art, but also its individual, component parts, can change the way we think about the Aztecs and how they may have structured their world. As Smith and Berdan state, "We feel that artistic expression, particularly in the form of stone sculpture and painted manuscripts, was a crucial component of the cultural context and ideology of the empire" (1996:7). It should be emphasized, however, that iconography was not merely a reflection of Aztec religion and society, but was actively utilized as a means of constructing, re-constructing, manipulating, and maintaining the ideology of self and empire in the Aztec world.

Bibliography

1966 *Codex Laud (Ms. Laud Misc. 678) Bodleian Library Oxford.* Codices Selecti XI. Akademische Druck- und Verlagsanstalt, Graz.

1993 *Codice Vaticano B.3773.* Codices Mexicanos. Fondo de Cultura Economica and Akademische Druck- und Verlagsanstalt., Mexico and Austria.

1994 *Codice Fejervary-Mayer.* Codices Mexicanos. Fondo de Cultura Economica and Akademische Druck- und Verlagsanstalt, Mexico and Austria.

Acosta, J. d.
2002 *Natural and Moral History of the Indies.* Duke University Press, Durham.

Aguilera Garcia, M. d. C.
1978 *Coyolxauhqui: Ensayo Iconográfico.* B.N.A.H.-I.N.A.H., México.

2001 *Coyolxauhqui: the Mexica Milky Way.* Labyrinthos, Lancaster.

Alcina Franch, J.
1995 Tláloc y los Tlaloques en los códices del México central. *Estudios de Cultura Nahuatl* 25:29-43.

Alcina Franch, J., M. León-Portilla and E. Matos Moctezuma (editors)
1992 *Azteca Mexica.* Sociedad Estatal Quinto Centenario., Madrid.

Araujo, C. R. M.
1945 La Fiesta Azteca de la Cosecha Ochpanistli. *Anales del Instituto Nacional de Antropología* 1 (1939-40):157-174.

Arnold, P. P.
1999 *Eating Landscape: Aztec and European Occupation of Tlalocan.* University Press of Colorado, Niwot.

Baez-Jorge, F.
2000 *Los oficios de las diosas: Dialéctica de la religiosidad popular en los grupos indios de Mexico.* Universidad Veracruzana, México.

Baquedano, E.
1984 *Aztec Sculpture.* British Museum Publications, London.

1988 Aspects of Death Symbolism in Aztec Tlaltecuhtli. In *The Symbolism in the Plastic and Pictorial Representations of Ancient Mexico*, edited by J. de Durand-Forest and M. Eisinger. Holos, Bonn.

1989 Aztec Earth Deities. In *Polytheistic Systems*, edited by G. Davies. Edinburgh University Press., Edinburgh.

1990 The Mesoamerican Ballgame: Symbolic Aspects. In *Contests*, edited by A. Duff-Cooper. Edinburgh University Press, Edinburgh.

Baquedano, E. and M. Graulich
1993 Decapitation among the Aztecs: Mythology, Agriculture and Politics, and Hunting. *Estudios de Cultura Nahuatl* 23:163-178.

Baquedano, E. and C. Orton
1990 Similarities between sculptures using Jaccard's coefficient in the study of Aztec Tlaltecuhtli. *Papers from the Institute of Archaeology*:16-23.

Batres, L.
1900 *Excavations in Escalerillas Street, City of Mexico*. J. Aguilera Vera and Co., Mexico.

Berlo, J. C.
1988 Icons and Ideologies at Teotihuacan: The Great Goddess Reconsidered. In *Art, Ideology, and the City of Teotihuacan*, edited by J. C. Berlo. Dumbarton Oaks Research Library and Collection, Washington, D.C.

Berrin, K. and E. Pasztory (editors)
1993 *Teotihuacan: Art from the City of the Gods*. The Fine Arts Museums of San Francisco, San Francisco.

Beyer, H.
1933 Shell Ornament Sets from the Huasteca, Mexico. *Studies in Middle America* 5(4):153-215.

Bierhorst, J. (editor)
1992 *Codex Chimalpopoca: the text in Nahuatl with a glossary and grammatical notes*. University of Arizona Press, Tucson.

Bonifaz Nuño, R.
1986 *Imagen de Tláloc: Hipótesis Iconográfica y Textual*. Universidad Autónoma de México, México.

Boone, E. H.
1983 *The Codex Magliabechiano and the Lost Prototype of the Magliabechiano Group: Commentary and Facsimile*. University of California Press, Los Angeles.

1999 The "Coatlicues" at the Templo Mayor. *Ancient Mesoamerica* 10:189-206.

Broda, J.
1983 The Provenience of the Offerings: Tribute and Cosmovision. In *The Aztec Templo Mayor*, edited by E. H. Boone. Dumbarton Oaks Research Library and Collection, Washington, D.C.

1987 Templo Mayor as Ritual Space. In *The Great Temple of Tenochtitlan: Center and Periphery in the Aztec World*, edited by J. Broda, D. Carrasco and E. Matos Moctezuma. University of California Press, Berkley.

Brumfiel, E. M.
1991 Weaving and Cooking: Women's Production in Aztec Mexico. In *Engendering Archaeology: Women and Prehistory*, edited by M. Conkey and J. M. Gero. Basil Blackwell, Oxford.

1996 Figurines and the Aztec State: Testing the Effectiveness of Ideological Domination. In *Gender and Archaeology*, edited by R. P. Wright. University of Pennsylvania Press, Philadelphia.

Brundage, B. C.
1972 *A Rain of Darts, The Mexico Aztecs*. University of Texas Press, Austin.

1979 *The Fifth Sun: Aztec Gods, Aztec World*. University of Texas Press, Austin.

Carrasco, D.
1987 Myth, Cosmic Terror, and the Templo Mayor. In *The Great Temple of Tenochtitlan: Center and Periphery in the Aztec World*, edited by J. Broda, D. Carrasco and E. Matos Moctezuma. University of California Press, Los Angeles.

1990 *Religions of Mesoamerica: Cosmovision and Ceremonial Centers*. Harper and Row, San Francisco.

Carrasco, D. and S. Sessions
1998 *Daily Life of the Aztecs: People of the Sun and Earth*. Greenwood Press, Westport.

Carrera, M. M.
1979 *The Representation of Women in Aztec-Mexica Sculpture*. Dissertation, Columbia University.

Caso, A.

1927 *El Teocalli de la Guerra Sagrada: Descripción y Estudio del Monolito Encontrado en los Cimientos del Palacio Nacional*. Talleras Gráficos de la Nación, México.

1945 *La Religión de los Aztecas*. Secretaria de Educación Pública, México.

1966 Dioses y Signos Teotihuacanos. In *Teotihuacan: Onceava Mesa Redonda*. Sociedad Mexicana de Antropología, México.

1970 *The Aztecs: People of the Sun*. Translated by L. Dunham. University of Oklahoma Press, Norman.

Conkey, M. and J. M. Gero

1991 Tensions, Pluralities, and Engendering Archaeology: An Introduction to Women and Prehistory. In *Engendering Archaeology: Women and Prehistory*, edited by M. Conkey and J. M. Gero, pp. 3-30. Basil Blackwell, Oxford.

Covarrubias, M.

1971 *Indian Art of Mexico and Central America*. Third ed. Alfred A. Knopf, New York.

Diaz del Castillo, B.

1927 *The True History of The Conquest of Mexico*. Translated by M. Keatinge 1. Robert M. McBride and Company., New York.

Diaz, G., and Alan Rodgers

1993 *The Codex Borgia: A Full-Color Restoration of the Ancient Mexican Manuscript*. Dover Publications, Inc., New York.

Durán, F. D.

1971 *Book of the Gods and Rites and the Ancient Calendar*. Translated by F. Horcasitas and D. Heyden. University of Oklahoma Press, Norman.

1994 *History of the Indies of New Spain*. Translated by D. Heyden. University of Oklahoma Press, Norman.

Fox, J. G.

1993 The Ballcourt Markers of Tenam Rosario, Chiapas, Mexico. *Ancient Mesoamerica* 4:55-64.

Fradcourt, A.

1993 New Insights on the Interpretation of the Aztec Calendar Stone. In *The Symbolism in the Plastic and Pictorial Representations of Ancient Mexico*, edited by J. de Durand-Forest and M. Eisinger. Holos, Bonn.

Furst, P. T.

1972 Symbolism and Psychopharmacology: the Toad as Earth Mother in Indian America. In *Religión en Mesoamérica. XII Mesa Redonda*, edited by J. L. King and N. C. Tejero. Sociedad Mexicana de Antropología, México.

Gailey, C. W.

1985 The State of the State in Anthropology. *Dialectical Anthropology* 9:65-89.

Garibay, A. M.

1970 *Llave de Nahuatl: Coleccion de trozos clásicos, con gramática y vocabulario, para utilidad de los principiantes*. Third ed. Editorial Porrua, S.A., México.

1973 *Teogonía e Historia de los Mexicanos: Tres Opúsculos del Siglo XVI*. Editorial Porrua, S.A., México.

Gendrop, P.

1971 Las Higueras y los Murals Totonacas. In *Artes de Mexico*, pp. 48-53. vol. 18.

Gillespie, S.

1989 *The Aztec Kings: The Construction of Rulership in Mexico History*. University of Arizona Press, Tucson.

1991 Ballgames and Boundaries. In *The Mesoamerican Ballgame*, edited by V. L. Scarborough and D. R. Wilcox. University of Arizona Press, Tucson.

Girard, R.
1966 *Los Mayas: su civilización, su historia, sus vinculaciones continentales*. Libro Mex, México.

González Torres, Y.
1985 *El Sacrificio Humano Entre Los Mexicas*. Instituto Nacional de Antropología e Historia, Fondo de Cultura Económica, Mexico.

Graulich, M.
1983 Myths of Paradise Lost in Pre-Hispanic Central Mexico. *Current Anthropology* 24(5):575-588.

1988 Double Immolations in Ancient Mexican Sacrificial Ritual. *History of Religions* 27(4):393-404.

1991 Les grandes statues azteques dites de Coatlique et de Yollotlicue. In In *Cultures et sociétés Andes et Méso-Amérique: Mélanges en hommage à Pierre Duviols*, edited by R. Thiercelin. Universite de Provence, Provence.

1997 *Myths of Ancient Mexico*. Translated by B. Ortiz de Montellano and T. Ortiz de Montellano. University of Oklahoma Press, Norman.

Guiteras-Holmes, C.
1961 *Perils of the Soul: The World View of a Tzotzil Indian*. The Free Press of Glencoe, Inc., New York.

Gutiérrez Solana, N.
1983 *Objetos Ceremoniales en Piedra de la Cultura Mexica*. Universidad Nacional Autónoma de México, México.

1990 Relieve del Templo Mayor con Tláloc Tlaltecuhtli y Tláloc. *Anales del Instituto de Investigaciones Estéticas* 61:15-35.

Hellmuth, N. M.
1975 The Escuintla Hoards: Teotihuacan Art in Guatemala. *F.L.A.A.R. Progress Reports* 1(2).

1978 Teotihuacan Art in the Escuintla, Guatemala, Region. In *Middle Classic Mesoamerica: a.d. 400-700*, edited by E. Pasztory. Columbia University Press, New York.

Heyden, D.
1971 Comentarios sobre la Coatlicue recuperada durante las excavaciones realizadas para la construcción del Metro. *Anales del Instituto Nacional de Antropología e Historia* 50:153-170.

1974 La diosa madre: Itzpapalotl. *Boletín, Instituto Nacional de Antropología e Historia* 11 (Epoca II):3-14.

1976 Caves, Gods, and Myths: World-view and Planning in Teotihuacan. In *Mesoamerican Sites and World-Views*, edited by E. P. Benson. Dumbarton Oaks Research Library and Collections, Washington, D.C.

Houston, S. and D. Stuart
1996 Of gods, glyphs, and kings: divinity and rulership among the Classic Maya. *Antiquity* 70(268):289-312.

Joyce, R. A.
2000 *Gender and Power in Prehispanic Mesoamerica*. University of Texas Press, Austin.

Kampen, M. E.
1972 *The Sculptures of El Tajín, Veracruz, Mexico*. University of Florida Press, Gainesville.

Kellogg, S.
1988 Cognatic Kinship and Religion: Women in Aztec Society. In *Smoke and Mist: Mesoamerican Studies in Memory of Thelma D. Sullivan*, edited by J. K. Josserand and K. Dakin. B.A.R., Oxford.

Kerr, J.
1994 *The Maya Vase Book: a corpus of rollout photographs of Maya vases* 4. Kerr Associates, New York.

Klein, C.
1973 Post-Classic Mexican Death Imagery as a Sign of Cyclic Completion. In *Death and the Afterlife in Pre-Columbian America*, edited by E. P. Benson. Dumbarton Oaks Research Library and Collections, Washington, D.C.

1976 *The Face of the Earth: frontality in two-dimensional Mesoamerican art.* Garland Publishers, New York.

1977 The Identity of the Central Deity on the Aztec Calendar Stone. In *Pre-Columbian Art History*, edited by A. Cordy-Collins and J. Stern. Peek Publications, Palo Alto.

1980 Who was Tlaloc? *Journal of Latin American Lore* 6(2):155-204.

1988 Rethinking Cihuacoatl: Aztec Political Imagery of the Conquered Woman. In *Smoke and Mist: Mesoamerican Studies in Memory of Thelma D. Sullivan*, edited by J. K. Josserand and K. Dakin. B.A.R., Oxford.

1993 The Shield Woman: Resolution of an Aztec Gender Paradox. In *Current Topics in Aztec Studies, Essays in Honor of Dr. H.B. Nicholson*, edited by A. Cordy-Collins and D. Sharon. San Diego Museum of Man, San Diego.

1994 Fighting with Femininity: Gender and War in Aztec Mexico. *Estudios de Cultura Nahuatl* 24:219-253.

2000 The Devil and the Skirt: An iconographic inquiry into the pre-Hispanic nature of the tzitzimime. *Ancient Mesoamerica* 11:1-26.

2001 *Gender in Prehispanic America.* Dumbarton Oaks Research Library and Collections, Washington, D.C.

Koontz, R. A.
1994 *The iconography of El Tajín, Veracruz, Mexico.* . Dissertation, University of Texas at Austin.

Krickeberg, W.
1961 *Las Antiguas Culturas Mexicanas.* Second ed. Translated by S. Garst and J. Reuter. Fondo de Cultura Economica, Mexico.

Kubler, G.
1967 *The Iconography of the Art of Teotihuacan.* Studies in Pre-Columbian Art and Archaeology, no.4. Dumbarton Oaks Trustees for Harvard University, Washington, D.C.

Lehman, W.
1966 Las cinco mujeres de oeste muertas en el parto y los cinco dioses del sur en la mitología mexicana. In *Tradicciones Mesoamericanistas 1.* Sociedad Mexicana de Antropología, México.

León-Portilla, M.
1963 *Aztec Thought and Culture: A Study of the Ancient Nahuatl Mind.* Translated by J. E. Davis. Civilization of the American Indian Series. University of Oklahoma Press, Norman.

López Austín, A.
1988 *The Human Body and Ideology, Concepts of the Ancient Nahuas.* Translated by B. Ortiz de Montellano and T. Ortiz de Montellano 1. University of Utah Press, Salt Lake City.

1990 *The Myths of the Opossum*. Translated by B. Ortiz de Montellano and T. Ortiz de Montellano. University of New Mexico Press, Albuquerque: .

López Luján, L.
1994 *The Offerings of the Templo Mayor of Tenochtitlan*. Translated by B. Ortiz de Montellano and T. Ortiz de Montellano. University Press of Colorado, Niwot.

Lupo, A.
1995 *La Tierra nos escucha: la cosmología de los nahuas a través de las súplicas rituales*. Consejo Nacional para la Cultura y las Artes: Instituto Nacional Indigenista, Mexico.

Madsen, W.
1960 *The Virgin's Children: Life in an Aztec Village Today*. University of Texas Press, Austin.

Matos Moctezuma, E.
1983 Symbolism of the Templo Mayor. In *The Aztec Templo Mayor*, edited by E. H. Boone. Dumbarton Oaks Research Library and Collection, Washington, D.C.

1984 The Templo Mayor of Tenochtitlan. In *Ritual Human Sacrifice in Mesoamerica*, edited by E. H. Boone. Dumbarton Oaks Research Library and Collection, Washington, D.C.

1987 The Templo Mayor of Tenochtitlan: History and Interpretation. In *The Great Temple of Tenochtitlan: Center and Periphery in the Aztec World*. University of California Press, Berkley.

1991 Las Seis Coyolxauhqui: Variaciones Sobre un Mismo Tema. *Estudios de Cultura Nahuatl* 21:2-29.

1995 *Life and Death in the Templo Mayor*. Translated by B. Ortiz de Montellano and T. Ortiz de Montellano. University Press of Colorado, Niwot.

1997 Tlaltecuhtli: Señor de la Tierra. *Estudios de Cultura Nahuatl* 27:15-40.

Matos Moctezuma, E. and F. Solís (editors)
2002 *Aztecs*. Royal Academy of Arts, London.

McCafferty, S. D. and G. G. McCafferty
1988 Powerful Women and the Myth of Male Dominance in Aztec Society. *Archaeological review from Cambridge* 7(1):45-59.

1991 Spinning and Weaving as Female Gender Identity in Post-Classic Mexico. In *Textile Traditions of Mesoamerica and the Andes: An Anthology*, pp. 19-44. Garland, New York.

Mendieta, G. d.
1945 *Historia Eclesiástica Indiana; Obra escrita a fines del siglo XVI* 1. Editorial Salvador Chavez Hayho, Mexico.

Milbrath, S.
1988 Birth Images in Mixteca-Puebla Art. In *The Role of Gender in Precolumbian Art and Architecture*, edited by V. E. Miller. University Press of America, Lanham.

1995 Gender and Roles of Lunar Deities in Postclassic Central Mexico and Their Correlations with the Maya Area. *Estudios de Cultura Nahuatl* 25:45-93.

Miller, M. and K. Taube
1993 *An Illustrated Dictionary of the Gods and Symbols of Ancient Mexico and the Maya*. Thames and Hudson, London.

Miller, V. E.
1988 The Role of Gender in Precolumbian Art and Architecture: Introduction. In *The Role of Gender in Precolumbian Art and Architecture*, edited by V. E. Miller. University Press of America, Lanham.

Motolinía, T.
1970 *Memoriales a Historia de los Indios de la Nueva España. Vol. 240.* Atlas., Madrid.

Nash, J.
1978 The Aztecs and the Ideology of Male Dominance. *Signs* 4(2):349-362.

1980 Aztec Women: The Transition from Status to Class in Empire and Colony. In *Women and Colonization: Anthropological Perspectivs*, edited by M. Etienne and E. Leacock. Bergin and Garvey Publishers, Inc., New York.

1997 Gendered Deities and the Survival of Culture. *History of Religions* 36(4):333-356.

Nicholson, H. B.
1954 The Birth of the Smoking Mirror. *Archaeology* 7(3):164-170.

1967 A Fragment of an Aztec Relief Carving of the Earth Monster. *Journal de la Société des Americanistes* 56(1):81-89.

1971 Religion in Pre-Hispanic Central Mexico. *Handbook of Middle American Indians* 10:395-446.

1972 The Iconography of Aztec Period Representations of the Earth Monster: Tlaltecuhtli. In *Religión en Mesoamérica. XII Mesa Redonda*, edited by J. L. King and N. C. Tejero. Sociedad Mexicana de Antropologia, Mexico.

1993 The Problem of the Identification of the Central Image of the "Aztec Calendar Stone". In *Current Topics in Aztec Studies, Essays in Honor of Dr. H.B. Nicholson*, edited by A. Cordy-Collins and D. Sharon. San Diego Museum of Man, San Diego.

Nicholson, H. B. and E. Quinones Keber
1983 *Art of Aztec Mexico: Treasures of Tenochtitlan.* National Gallery of Art, Washington, D.C.

Nuttall, Z.
1901 *The Fundamental Principles of Old and New World Civilizations: a comparative research based on a study of the ancient Mexican religious, sociological, and calendrical systems.* Peabody Museum Papers II. Peabody Museum of American Archaeology and Ethnology, Cambridge.

1975 *The Codex Nuttall: A Picture Manuscript from Ancient Mexico; The Peabody Museum Facsimile Edited by Zelia Nuttall.* Dover, New York.

Pasztory, E.
1972 The Gods of Teotihuacan: a Synthetic Approach in Teotihuacan Iconography. *Atti del XL Congresso Internazionale degli Americanisti.*

1974 *The Iconography of the Teotihuacan Tlaloc.* Studies in Pre-Columbian Art and Architecture, no.15. Dumbarton Oaks Trustees for Harvard University, Washington, D.C.

1983 *Aztec Art.* Henry A. Abrams, New York.

1988 The Aztec Tlaloc: God of Antiquity. In *Smoke and Mist: Mesoamerican Studies in Memory of Thelma D. Sullivan*, edited by J. K. Josserand and K. Dakin. B.A.R., Oxford.

1997 *Teotihuacan: An Experiment in Living.* University of Oklahoma Press, Norman.

Paulinyi, Z.
2001 Los Señores con Tocado de Borlas: un estudio sobre el estado teotihuacano. *Ancient Mesoamerica* 12(1):1-30.

Peterson, J. F.
1983 Sacrificial Earth: The Iconography and Function of Malinalli Grass in Aztec Culture. In *Flora and Fauna Imagery in Precolumbian Cultures: Iconography and Function*, edited by N. Hammond. B.A.R., Oxford.

Piña Chán, B. B. d. (editor)
1998 *Iconografia Mexicana*. Instituto Nacional de Antropologia e Historia, Mexico.

Piña Chán, R., and Patricia Castillo Peña
1999 *Tajín: La ciudad del dios Huracán*. Fondo de Cultura Económica, Mexico.

Proskouriakoff, T.
1950 Varieties of Classic Central Veracruz Sculpture. *Contributions to American Anthropology and History* 12(58):61-94.

1968 The Jog and the Jaguar Signs in Maya Writing. *American Antiquity* 33(2):247-251.

Quezada, N.
1977 Creencias Tradicionales Sobre Embarazo y Parto. *Anales de Antropología* 14:307-326.

Quinones Keber, E.
1995 *Codex Telleriano-Remensis: Ritual, Divination, and History in a Pictorial Aztec Manuscript*. University of Texas Press, Austin.

Redfield, R. and A. Villa Rojas
1934 *Chan Kom, a Maya village*. Carnegie Institution of Washington, Washington, D.C.

Robicsek, F. and D. M. Hales
1984 Maya Heart Sacrifice: Cultural Perspective and Surgical Technique. In *Ritual Human Sacrifice in Mesoamerica*, edited by E. H. Boone. Dumbarton Oaks Research Library and Collection, Washington, D.C.

Rodríguez Valdés, M. J.
1988 *La Mujer Azteca*. Universidad Autónoma del Estado de México, México.

Roscoe, W.
1991 *The Zuni Man-Woman*. University of New Mexico Press, Albuquerque.

Rowe, J. H.
1977 Form and Meaning in Chavín Art. In *Pre-Columbian Art History: Selected Readings*, edited by A. Cordy-Collins and J. Stern. Peek Publications, Palo Alto.

Ruiz de Alarcón, H.
1984 *Treatise on the Heathen Superstitions That Today Live Among the Indians Native to This New Spain, 1629*. Translated by J. R. Andrews and R. Hassig. University of Oklahoma Press, Norman.

Sahagún, F. B. d.
1950-1982 *Florentine Codex: General History of the Things of New Spain*. 12 vols. School of American Research., Santa Fe.

1958 *Veinte Himnos Sacros de los Nahuas; Los recogio de los nativos F. Bernadino de Sahagun, Franciscano*. Translated by A. M. Garibay. Fuentes Indígenas de la Cultura Nahuatl, Informantes de Sahagun, 2. Universidad Nacional Autónoma de México, México.

1997 *Primeros Memoriales*. Translated by T. D. Sullivan. University of Oklahoma Press, Norman.

Sandstrom, A. R.
1991 *Corn is Our Blood: Culture and Ethnic Identity in a Contemporary Aztec Indian Village*. University of Oklahoma Press, Norman.

Saturno, W. A., K. Taube and D. Stuart
2005 *Los murales de San Bartolo, El Petén, Guatemala (Part I. El mural del norte)*. Ancient America 7. Center for Ancient American Studies, Barnardsville.

Schaefer, S.
1989 The Loom and Time in the Huichol World. *Journal of Latin American Lore* 15(2):179-194.

Schele, L. and M. Miller
1986 *The Blood of Kings: Dynasty and Ritual in Maya Art*. George Braziller, New York.

Seler, E.
1963 *Commentarios al Codice Borgia*. Translated by M. Frenk. Fondo de Cultura Económica, México.

1990- *Collected Works in Mesoamerican linguistics and archaeology*. Second ed. 6 vols. Labyrinthos, Culver City.

Shelton, A.
1989 Preliminary Notes on some Structural Parallels in the Symbolic and Relational Classifications of Nahuatl and Huichol Deities. In *Polytheistic Systems*, edited by G. Davies. Edinburgh University Press, Edinburgh.

Simeon, R.
1977 *Diccionario de la lengua Nahuatl o mexicana*. Translated by J. O. de Coll. Siglo Veintiuno., México.

Smith, M. E. and F. F. Berdan
1996 Introduction. In *Aztec Imperial Strategies*, edited by F. F. Berdan, R. E. Blanton, E. H. Boone, M. G. Hodge, M. E. Smith and E. Umberger. Dumbarton Oaks Research Library and Collection, Washington, D.C.

Solís, F.
1998 *Tesoros Artísticos del Museo Nacional de Antropología*. Instituto Nacional de Antropología e Historia, México.

2004 *The Aztec Empire*. Guggenheim Museum Publications, New York.

Stone, A.
1989 Disconnection, Foreign Insignia, and Political Expansion: Teotihuacan and the Warrior Stelae of Piedras Negras. In *Mesoamerica after the decline of Teotihuacan, A.D. 700-900*, edited by R. A. Diehl and J. C. Berlo. Dumbarton Oaks Research Library and Collection, Washington, DC.

Sullivan, T. D.
1972 Tlaloc: A new etymological interpretation of the God's name and what it reveals of his essence and nature. *Atti del XL Congresso Internazionale Degli Americanisti: Tilgher*.

1982 Tlazolteotl-Ixcuina: The Great Spinner and Weaver. In *The Art and Iconography of Late Post-Classic Central Mexico*, edited by E. H. Boone. Dumbarton Oaks Trustees for Harvard University, Washington, D.C.

Taube, K. A.
1983 The Teotihuacan Spider Woman. *Journal of Latin American Lore* 9(2):107-189.

1986 The Teotihuacan Cave of Origin. *RES* 12:51-82.

1992 The Iconography of Mirrors at Teotihuacan. In *Art, Ideology, and the City of Teotihuacan*, edited by J. C. Berlo. Dumbarton Oaks, Washington, D.C.

1993a *Aztec and Maya Myths*. University of Texas Press, Austin.

1993b The Bilimek Pulque Vessel: Starlore, Calendrics, and Cosmology in Late Postclassic Central Mexico. *Ancient Mesoamerica* 4:1-15.

1994 The Birth Vase: Natal Imagery in Ancient Maya Myth and Ritual. In *The Maya Vase Book*, edited by B. Kerr and J. Kerr. vol. 4. Kerr Associates, New York.

1998 The Mirrors of Offerings 1 and 2 of Sala 2 in the Palacio Quemado at Tula: an Iconographic Interpretation.

2004 Aztec Religion: Creation, Sacrifice, and Renewal. In *The Aztec Empire*, edited by F. Solís. Guggenheim Museum Publications, New York.

Tezózomoc, H. A.
1975 *Crónica Mexicanayotl*. Translated by A. Leon. Universitaria, México.

1987 *Crónica Mexicana*. Fourth ed. Editorial Porrua, S.A., México.

Thompson, J. E. S.
1943 Representations of Tlalchitonatiuh at Chichen Itza, Yucatan, and at Baul, Escuintla. *Notes on Middle American Archaeology and Ethnology* 1(19):117-121.

1960 *Maya Hieroglyphic Writing: An Introduction*. University of Oklahoma Press, Norman.

1970 *Maya History and Religion*. University of Oklahoma Press, Norman.

Townsend, R. F.
1979 *State and Cosmos in the Art of Tenochtitlan*. Studies in Pre-Columbian Art and Archaeology, no.20. Dumbarton Oaks Trustees for Harvard University., Washington, D.C.

Umberger, E.
1981 *Aztec Sculptures, Hieroglyphs, and History*. Dissertation, Columbia University.

1996 Art and Imperial Strategy in Tenochtitlan. In *Aztec Imperial Strategies*, edited by F. F. Berdan, R. E. Blanton, E. H. Boone, M. G. Hodge, M. E. Smith and E. Umberger. Dumbarton Oaks Research Library and Collection, Washington, D.C.

Van Zantwijk, R.
1985 *The Aztec Arrangement: the Social History of Pre-Spanish Mexico*. University of Oklahoma Press, Norman.

Von Winning, H.
1968 *Pre-Columbian Art of Mexico and Central America*. Harry N. Abrams, Inc., New York.

1987 *La Iconografía de Teotihuacan: Los Dioses y Los Signos*. 2 vols. Universidad Nacional Autónoma de Mexico, México.

Wilkerson, S. J.
1984 In Search of the Mountain of Foam: Human Sacrifice in Eastern Mesoamerica. In *Ritual Human Sacrifice in Mesoamerica*, edited by E. H. Boone. Dumbarton Oaks Research Library and Collection, Washington, D.C.

1991 And Then They Were Sacrificed. In *The Mesoamerican Ballgame*, edited by V. L. Scarborough and D. R. Wilcox. University of Arizona Press., Tucson.

Zingg, R. M.
1977 *Report of the Mr. and Mrs. Henry Pfeiffer Expedition for Huichol Ethnography: the Huichols, primitive artists*, Millwood: Kraus Reproduction Co.

www.ingramcontent.com/pod-product-compliance
Lightning Source LLC
LaVergne TN
LVHW070534110826
845147LV00017BA/986
* 9 7 8 1 4 0 7 3 0 0 8 3 2 *